M000195838

A
South Carolina
Chronology
1497–1992
Second Edition

A South Carolina Chronology 1497–1992

Second Edition

George C. Rogers, Jr.
and
C. James Taylor

University of South Carolina Press

Library of Congress Cataloging-in-Publication Data

Rogers, George C.
  A South Carolina chronology, 1497–1992 / George C. Rogers, Jr. and
C. James Taylor. — 2nd ed.
      p.   cm.
  Includes bibliographical references and index.
  ISBN 0–87249–971–5 (alk. paper)
  1. South Carolina—History—Chronology.   I. Taylor, C. James,
1945– .   II. Title.
F269.R675   1993
975.7′002′02—dc20   93–27306

Contents

PREFACE   vii

I. ESTABLISHING EUROPEAN CLAIMS
(1497–1669)   1

II. THE COLONY (1670–1764)   8

III. REVOLUTION (1765–1790)   38

IV. THE STATE AND THE UNION
(1791–1859)   63

V. SECESSION, WAR, AND AFTER
(1860–1895)   94

VI. THE SEGREGATED STATE (1896–1964)   115

VII. THE MODERN STATE (1965–1992)   141

INDEX   155

Preface

These are the principal dates in the history of South Carolina. The compilers have tried to incorporate events that would reflect the total history of the province and the state so that if one read through the chronology one would be aware of the fundamental developments in Carolina society and the major changes that have occurred.

The second edition of *A South Carolina Chronology* has been necessitated by the changes that have occurred in the focus of American history over the last twenty years. In addition to the new broader reading of events that expands the previously chronicled period to take more notice of race, gender, and other social issues, twenty years of notable changes and remarkable events have added measurably to South Carolina's history and this chronology.

If this work is updated again in the next century almost certainly the focus will have changed, new questions will be asked, and serious omissions will be found. And, of course, another generation of the state's history will need to be chronicled. Readers are admonished, as in the 1973 edition, to report errors and omissions to be kept on file for that inevitable revision.

George C. Rogers, Jr.

C. James Taylor

A
South Carolina
Chronology
1497–1992
Second Edition

I. ESTABLISHING EUROPEAN CLAIMS (1497–1669)

The foothills and coastal plain bounded on the south by the Savannah River, on the west by the Appalachian Mountains, and on the east by the Atlantic Ocean, make up the territory we now call South Carolina. The state has no major natural boundary to the north until one comes to the Roanoke River, which debouches into the Albemarle Sound around latitude 36 north. The region is curiously divided into a geologically very ancient area of Precambrian rock formations, of which the blue granite quarried in Fairfield County is an example, and a flat southeastern area where sand, shells, and marl were deposited in the relatively recent Cretaceous period.

We know very little about the Native Americans who lived here before European settlement. Each year new archeological discoveries are made, and we learn more about the first inhabitants of this area. The perspective of our globe has changed drastically in the past two decades as the theory of plate tectonics has been accepted. The continents do float on the mantle of the earth. Pangaea is the concept of the first land masses when they were all nestled together. Since that time the seven continents have drifted apart until they took the configuration that they make today on the globe. Homo sapiens emerged long ago in Asia and Africa and from those origins these early people have spread across the global land masses. It is agreed that the Native Americans crossed a Bering Sea land bridge about 15,000 years ago from Asia to North America. These were the ancestors of the Incas, the Mayans, the Aztecs, and all of the Indian tribes that have figured in the history of what is now the United States and of South Carolina. One feature of their cultures shared throughout the inhabited "new world" was

1

the building of mounds for ceremonial and religious purposes. The most exciting remains are the temples of Central America. In what is now the U.S. we speak of the Mississippian culture with the chief example that of Cahokia in present-day Illinois. At least the largest mounds have been found at that site. There are lesser configurations at Ocmulgee and Muscogee in Georgia and Cofitachiqui on the Wateree River just south of Camden, South Carolina.

The major Native American groups in what has become the state of South Carolina were the Iroquoian, Algonquian, Muskhogean, Siouan, and Cusabo peoples. At the time of the entrance of the Europeans—Spanish, French, and English—these natives were organized into chiefdoms, the hierarchy of which has been best delineated by archaeologist Charles Hudson and his students. The Cacique of Kiawah and the Queen of Confitachiqui are the best known examples.

1497 John Cabot sailed from Bristol for the new world on May 20, made his landfall near the northern tip of Newfoundland on June 24, and returned to Bristol on August 6. By this remarkably swift voyage, England secured a claim to the title of all of North America by right of discovery.

1521 Lucas Vásquez de Ayllón sent an expedition from Santo Domingo which explored the Florida coast as far north as thirty-three degrees thirty minutes, thereby making a claim in the name of the king of Spain to an area which would have included present-day Carolina.

1524 Giovanni da Verrazzano, commissioned by the king of France to explore the new world, sighted land in March just north of what is now Myrtle Beach before sailing northward in quest of the western sea.

1526 Ayllón made the first European settlement in what is now South Carolina at San Miguel de Gualdape, which is presumed to have been on the east bank of the Waccamaw River, opposite present-day Georgetown, although others now think it was located further south. The Spaniards called the land Chicora. The initial population of the settlement was approximately 600, including a number of black slaves from Santo Domingo.

October 18. Ayllón died.

November. The slaves at San Miguel de Gualdape mutinied. This was the first black slave revolt in North America although there were probably recently-captured Siouan Indians also involved.

1527 *About January.* Disheartened by disease, famine, the death of their leader, the slave revolt, and an unusually severe winter, the surviving settlers left San Miguel. About 150 of them reached Santo Domingo.

1540 *April.* Coming from the south, Hernando de Soto after crossing the Savannah River reached an Indian settlement called Confitachiqui, which recent study places on the Wateree River south of Camden.

May 3. De Soto left Confitachiqui and made his way across the mountains, probably by way of the French Broad and Tennessee rivers.

1562 *May.* Jean Ribaut and his band of Huguenots planted a settlement, which he called Charlesfort, in the vicinity of Parris Island. He named the region Carolus in honor of Charles IX of France and gave the name Port Royal to the sound that still bears that name.

June 11. Ribaut sailed home, leaving behind about thirty men who soon became desperate. Believing themselves to have been forgotten, they sailed to Europe in a makeshift vessel and were forced to turn to cannibalism when food ran out.

1564 René de Laudonnière and a second group of French Huguenots settled near the mouth of the St. John's River in Florida and built Fort Caroline.

1565 *September 8.* The Spaniard Pedro Menéndez de Avilés took possession of the first site of St. Augustine, Florida, which became the center of Spanish influence south of Carolina and, in the eighteenth century, the great rival of Charles Town.

September 29. Menéndez massacred the French after the capture of Fort Caroline.

1566 *April.* Menéndez built the Spanish outpost known as Fort San Felipe on Parris Island.

November. Menéndez sent Juan Pardo to explore the hinterland of Fort San Felipe. Pardo reached the mountains.

1567 Pardo again explored the interior following a route paralleling that of de Soto.

1576 *July.* Native Americans demolished Fort San Felipe and forced the Spaniards to retreat to St. Augustine. The attackers may have been Westos but probably were Muskhogeans who had either been enslaved by the Spaniards or had been accepted into the fort as Christian converts.

1577 The Spaniards returned to build San Marcos not far from where Fort San Felipe had stood. Spanish missions, along the coast from St. Augustine as far north at least as the South Edisto River, survived until 1686.

1629 *October 30.* Charles I of England granted to his attorney general Sir Robert Heath the territory in America between thirty-one and thirty-six degrees north latitude. This land, which extended from the northern limits of modern Florida to Albemarle Sound and from ocean to ocean, was to be called Carolana in honor of King Charles I.

1660 *May 8.* Charles II was proclaimed king of England in Westminster Hall, London.

1663 *March 24.* Charles II granted the territory which had been called Carolana to Edward Hyde (Earl of Clarendon), George Monck (Duke of Albemarle), William Craven (Earl of Craven), John Berkeley (Baron Berkeley of Stratton), Anthony Ashley Cooper (Baron Ashley of Wimborne St. Giles), Sir George Carteret, Sir William Berkeley, and Sir John Colleton, who were designated "the true and absolute Lords and Proprietaries" of what was now to be known as Carolina.

August 26. Captain William Hilton, who had sailed from Barbados on August 10 to explore the new grant in the names of the Lords Proprietors, reached the coast of Carolina and probed the creeks and rivers around the island now called Hilton Head. He returned to Barbados on January 6, 1664.

1664   *May 29.* The Barbadians made a short-lived settlement on the Cape Fear River. Sir John Yeamans was appointed governor of this colony, the county of Clarendon.

1665   *January 7.* The *Concessions and Agreements* between the Lords Proprietors and William Yeamans, the son of Sir John, and others contained provisions for governing and distributing land in Carolina.

June 30. A second charter was granted to the "Lords and Proprietaries" of Carolina in order to remove a possible defect in their title, arising from the fact that the 1663 charter had been issued prior to the order in council which declared the Heath grant of 1629 void. The new boundaries reached as far north as the present Virginia-North Carolina line and as far south as 100 miles below the present Georgia-Florida line.

1666   *June 14–July 12.* Captain Robert Sandford, secretary and chief register of the county of Clarendon (Cape Fear settlement), at the direction of Governor Yeamans explored the coast to the south of Cape Fear.

1667   *Autumn.* The county of Clarendon was abandoned.

1669   *July 21.* In England, Lord Ashley issued the Fundamental Constitutions, much influenced by the ideas of his secretary John Locke and perhaps by those of James Harrington. The adventurous settlers never accepted this or later versions of the Fundamental Constitutions, which are, however, generally felt to have influenced the character of the state as it developed. The Constitutions decreed that most governmental power would be in the hands of a landed gentry, for whom various titles were specified. This first version allowed an unusually large degree of religious toleration.

August. The *Carolina,* the *Port Royal,* and the *Albemarle* sailed from England with 100 colonists under the command of Joseph West, who later emerged as the ablest of the early leaders of the colony, serving as governor three times.

September 17. Soon after this date the three ships left Kinsale, Ireland, where additional settlers had been taken on.

Late October. The three ships reached Barbados.

November 2. A storm wrecked the *Albemarle* but the passengers and crew were rescued.

II. THE COLONY
(1670–1764)

After difficult beginnings, the settlement at Charles Town suddenly began to boom when the pirates unloaded their loot and the settlers opened up a trade in skins and furs with the Native Americans. About the same time (1685–1696) the terms "South Carolina" and "North Carolina" came into use. Although the two settlements were formally part of the same province, "Carolina," they were not only hundreds of miles apart (one around Albemarle Sound and the other at Charles Town), but also were very different from each other, and it was never practicable to administer them as one unit. North Carolina's early settlers were mostly immigrants from Virginia, and the coast north of Cape Fear was lacking in natural harbors. For a while (1692–1710) North Carolina was governed by deputies appointed by the governors of South Carolina who resided in Charles Town. North Carolina's prosperity came later when the hinterland was developed.

But South Carolina's early prosperity was bought at a terrible price. Greed overcame the moral scruples that some settlers surely had about owning slaves. Black slaves, imported at first from Barbados and then directly from Africa, were found to be more tractable workers in the rice fields after that crop was introduced in the 1690s and more resistant to malaria than Native Americans. By 1708 the number of blacks in the colony exceeded the number of whites and by 1730, excluding Native Americans, blacks seem to have constituted two-thirds of the population. After 1750, because of white immigration overland from Pennsylvania and Virginia, the proportion of whites in the population increased until the 1790s when the white population was again the majority.

Besides deerskins and rice, ship's supplies such as lumber, tar, and turpentine were also exported profitably. By the late 1740s indigo had become an important export, but cotton was not a significant crop until the 1790s.

During this period Charles Town became one of the wealthiest towns in North America, with a sophisticated social and cultural life, although it never acquired the official English status of a city. Sephardic Jews were accepted in South Carolina and usually enjoyed more freedom to practice their religion than was the case in many European countries, but, although Jews achieved prominent positions, they were never a large proportion of the population.

By 1735 Georgetown and Beaufort had become substantial settlements and were able to compete with Charles Town for trade.

1670 *January 12.* The *Port Royal* was wrecked in the Bahamas.

February. Sir John Yeamans appointed Colonel William Sayle of Bermuda as the first governor of Carolina. Sayle was seventy-nine years old.

February 26. Under command of Sayle, the *Carolina* and a newly acquired vessel, the *Three Brothers,* left Bermuda for the Carolina coast, with instructions from the Proprietors to establish a settlement at Port Royal.

March 1. In England, the second version of the Fundamental Constitutions was drawn up. Not ratified.

March 15. The settlers sighted land near Bulls Bay.

April. After exploring the coast southward to Port Royal Sound the settlers, at the suggestion of a local Indian chief, the Cacique of Kiawah, fixed upon Albemarle Point up the Ashley River for their first home.

Summer. The first public elections were held in Carolina for membership in the Council.

August 23. Captain Henry Brayne brought the first black slaves to English Carolina.

August. A Spanish attempt from St. Augustine to destroy the new English settlement failed. By the end of 1670, word reached America of the Treaty of Madrid (July 18, 1670), in which Spain recognized the existence of English settlements north of St. Augustine. The estimated population of the settlement was 155, of whom about 15 were black. The Native American population of what we now call South Carolina was probably between 20,000 and 50,000.

1671 Stephen Bull sent a roll of South Carolina-grown tobacco to the Proprietors.

March 4. Governor William Sayle died, having nominated Joseph West as his temporary successor.

July. South Carolina's first assembly, called a parliament, met.

1672 The Lords Proprietors sent a barrel of rice with other supplies aboard the *William & Ralph*. This may have been used as seed and marked the beginning of rice cultivation in South Carolina that would prosper after the 1680s with the introduction of Madagascar rice.

April 23. In England, Lord Ashley was named the first Earl of Shaftesbury.

1674 *August.* Sir John Yeamans died. Joseph West succeeded him as governor and continued as such until October 1682.

October. The Westo Indians were subdued and became allies.

1679 *December 17.* The Lords Proprietors ordered the site of the settlement to be moved from Albemarle Point to Oyster Point, which lay at the confluence of the Ashley and Cooper rivers, and to be named Charles Town.

1680 The estimated population of the colony, excluding tribal Indians, was 1,200 including approximately 200 blacks.

April 30. The first group of Huguenots arrived at Oyster Point in the *Richmond.*

1681 A Congregational church was formed by the dissenters in Charles Town.

1682 St. Philip's congregation organized with its first church erected at the current site of St. Michael's in Charles Town.

January 12. In England, the third version of the Fundamental Constitutions was drawn up. Not ratified.

May 10. The Lords Proprietors ordered three counties to be laid out: Craven to the north, Berkeley in the center, Colleton to the south.

August 17. In England, the fourth version of the Fundamental Constitutions was drawn up. Not ratified.

1683 *December 23.* Quaker leader George Fox addressed a letter to the Friends of Charles Town on Ashley Cooper River in Carolina. This is the first evidence of Quaker activity in South Carolina.

1684 *March.* The first Baptist congregation settled in South Carolina (on Cooper River near Charles Town) after fleeing Massachusetts.

November. A group of Scots, covenanters who had not fared well under the Restoration, settled Stuart's Town near present-day Beaufort.

1685 *February 6.* In England, James II ascended the throne. Thereafter royal authority became more evident in the colonies. Apparently rice was being grown commercially in Carolina, and George Muschamp, the first direct representative of royal authority in the colony, came to collect customs and enforce the navigation acts.

October 18. In France, Louis XIV revoked the Edict of Nantes, which had guaranteed the rights of Huguenots. About 1,500 of them emigrated to South Carolina in the next ten years.

1686 Medway became the home of the first Landgrave Thomas Smith, who is buried in the garden. The first house was destroyed in 1705. A brick house later built upon the first foundation still stands.

August 17. The Spaniards destroyed Stuart's Town.

1687 The Huguenot Church in Charles Town was organized.

1688 *December.* In England, "The Glorious Revolution" caused James II to flee to France.

1689 Albemarle County ceased to exist. The government of Carolina "north and east of Cape Fear" was established.

April 11. William of Orange became King William III of England.

May 7. King William's War began; it was the first of a succession of wars between England and France for domination in North America.

December 16. The Declaration of Rights, which had been accepted by William and Mary previously on February 13, was enacted by Parliament as the English Bill of Rights.

1690 *February 7.* The first South Carolina law relating solely to slavery was enacted.

September 20. A patent was granted to Peter Jacob Guerard for a pendulum engine that husked rice.

November 8. Phillip Ludwell was commissioned by the Lords Proprietors as governor of all "Carolina." By the end of this year it was the practice, sanctioned by the Lords Proprietors, for the Grand Council to meet in two houses, one of deputies appointed by the Proprietors and the other of representatives elected by the people. Thus began the bicameral legislature.

December. A parliament convened in Charles Town banished the tyrannical and inept governor James Colleton. He was succeeded by Seth Sothell, who had previously been governor in North Carolina.

1692 *April.* Phillip Ludwell arrived in Charles Town. He appointed a deputy to govern "north and east of Cape Fear." The northern colony continued to be governed by deputies from Charles Town until 1710.

1693 *May 11.* The Lords Proprietors declared the Fundamental Constitutions inoperative—a formal recognition of the colonists' refusal to implement the system.

1695 *August 17.* The Quaker John Archdale became governor and inaugurated a period of sound and relatively popular government.

December 5. A group of New Englanders left Dorchester, Massachusetts, for a place on the Ashley River which they named Dorchester. They celebrated their arrival with divine service on January 26, 1696.

1696 *March 16.* South Carolina's first comprehensive slave law was enacted. It was based on the Barbados slave code of 1688.

1697 The first Jews arrived in South Carolina.

September 20. King William's War ended with the Peace of Ryswick.

1698 A Church of England parochial library was established in Charles Town by the Society for the Propagation of Christian Knowledge.

February 24. A fire destroyed one-fourth of Charles Town.

April 11. In England, the fifth and final version of the Fundamental Constitutions was drawn up. Not ratified.

October 8. Afraid of the growing number of blacks who had been imported as slaves, the Assembly passed a law granting £13 to anyone who would bring into the province a white male servant.

1699 Middleburg, the oldest house still standing in South Carolina, was built of wood by Benjamin Simons on the Eastern Branch of the Cooper River.

August 29–November 1. About 160 people died in the first yellow fever epidemic.

1700 The estimated population of the province, excluding tribal Indians, was 5,500. The population of blacks is not known, but was probably about 2,400.

November 16. The Assembly voted a financial contribution to the Charles Town parochial library, thus making it the first public library in the country.

1702 *March 8.* In England, William III died and was succeeded by Queen Anne.

May. Queen Anne's War began an eleven-year struggle against France and Spain for power in North America. Word of the war's outbreak did not reach South Carolina until August 26.

November–December. Governor James Moore attacked St. Augustine. He failed to take the fort but burned the town.

December 25. The Reverend Samuel Thomas, the first missionary sent out by the recently established Society for the Propagation of the Gospel in Foreign Parts, reached Charles Town.

1703 *April.* Bills of credit were issued to the value of £6,000 to pay for the war against Florida (the first "paper money" issued).

May 6. In order to break up the brisk trade in Indian slaves, the Assembly placed a duty of twenty shillings per head on each Indian slave exported. Many were exported to the West Indies and to New England.

November. Anthony Aston, having accompanied Moore on his expedition and having also written a play about South Carolina, departed Charles Town.

1704 A map by Edward Crisp showed Charles Town as a walled city. Charles Town, Santa Fe, and St. Augustine were the only walled cities ever erected within the confines of the present United States.

January. Former Governor James Moore led his second expedition against Florida, attacking the Apalachee Indians. Only four white Carolinians lost their lives, but Spanish territories were seriously weakened.

May 5. Payment was made for a Sword of State which was used by Proprietary, Royal, and State governments until it disappeared in 1941.

1705 *September 29.* On this date Parliament placed rice on the list of enumerated goods, which meant that all rice being shipped to Europe must pass through an English port.

1706 *August.* Despite an epidemic of yellow fever, Governor Sir Nathaniel Johnson and Colonel William Rhett repulsed an attack on Charles Town by French and Spanish forces marching from Bulls Bay to the Wando River.

November 30. By an act of the Assembly, the Church of England was established in the province. Ten parishes were laid out: St. Philip's, Christ Church, St. Thomas's and St. Denis's, St. James's Santee, St. John's Berkeley, St. James's Goose Creek, St. Andrew's, St. Paul's, and St. Bartholomew's. A church was to be built in each parish at public expense. The first to be built was that of St. Andrew's which was begun in 1706.

1707 Thomas Nairne, appointed Indian agent by the Assembly, attempted to direct an enlightened policy towards the Native Americans. He was killed in the Yemassee War April 15, 1715.

Henrietta Dering Johnston, the first woman professional artist in the colonies and the first pastel artist in America, arrived in Charles Town.

May 1. The Act of Union between England and Scotland henceforth permitted Scots to settle and trade in Carolina on equal terms with the English.

October 25. Land grants reveal that by this date what had been Port Royal County was now known as Granville County. It extended along the north side of the Savannah River far into the backcountry.

1708 Governor Sir Nathaniel Johnson reported population figures that revealed a black majority in South Carolina for the first time.

Black slaves	4,100
Whites	4,080
Indian slaves	1,400
Total	9,580

1709 *May 7.* Fort Johnson (named for Sir Nathaniel Johnson) on Windmill Point on James Island was built by this date, as a guard of twelve men was henceforth posted there.

1710 Indian trade was placed under the control of nine commissioners appointed by the Assembly.

December 7. The Lords Proprietors decided to appoint a governor for North Carolina who would be "independent of the governor of Carolina." Edward Hyde became first governor of North Carolina in 1712. Henceforth, North Carolina was governed as a separate colony.

1711 *January 17.* The Lords Proprietors ordered that the town of Beaufort on Port Royal Sound be established to serve as an outlet for the naval stores produced in Granville and Colleton counties.

December. Colonel John Barnwell led an expedition into North Carolina which suppressed an uprising of the Tuscarora Indians.

1712   *June.* Colonel Barnwell returned to South Carolina and was henceforth known as "Tuscarora Jack."

June 7. The parish of St. Helena was laid out to contain all of Granville County.

December. Colonel James Moore, son of the former governor, led a second expedition against the Tuscaroras of North Carolina.

December 12. The common law of England was declared in force in South Carolina.

December 12. The Assembly passed an act to establish a free school in Charles Town—the beginning of public education in South Carolina.

1713   *March 25.* Colonel Moore decisively defeated the Tuscaroras.

April 11. The Treaty of Utrecht ended Queen Anne's War.

1715   *April 15.* The massacre of almost 100 white settlers near Port Royal began the Yemassee War. The white settlers, with the aid of forces that included free Indians, black slaves, and reinforcements from North Carolina, quelled an uprising of the Yemassees, Cheraws, Creeks, Shawnees, and other tribes, which had jeopardized the safety of the colony.

May. Governor Charles Craven defeated the Yemassees and Shawnees at Salkehatchie.

Winter. Fort Moore was begun on the east bank of the Savannah River in what is now Aiken County.

1716 *January 31.* A 300-man military force marched into Cherokee territory to gain their support against the Creeks. The result was the first treaty with the Cherokees, who became indispensable allies of the settlers against the Creeks.

June 13. The Yemassee lands were opened to settlers.

December 15. The Assembly passed an act which designated the parishes, instead of the counties, as the units for representation in the Assembly. The law was disallowed in England.

1717 Sir Robert Montgomery, who had conceived of the establishment of the Margravate of Azilia as a buffer to the southward of Carolina, published in London *A Discourse Concerning the deign'd Establishment of a New Colony to the South of Carolina, in the Most delightful Country of the Universe.*

May 22. Edward Thatch (Teach), the notorious pirate Blackbeard, threatened to murder several prisoners and destroy Charleston to coerce officials into sending him a chest of medicine.

November. A treaty signed in Charles Town with the Creeks formally ended the Yemassee War.

December 11. The parish of St. George's Dorchester was carved out of St. Andrew's.

1718 Congaree Fort, the first frontier post in central South Carolina, was established.

September 27. Colonel William Rhett defeated the pirates, of whom Stede Bonnet was the captain, in a naval battle in the Cape Fear River.

October 17. An act for the more speedy trial of pirates was passed in order to punish them quickly.

December 10. Stede Bonnet was hanged at White Point between high and low tide.

1719 *December 10.* The first step in the Revolution of 1719 (in which the Carolinians overthrew Proprietary rule) was taken when the Assembly transformed itself into a convention of the people.

December 21. The convention proclaimed James Moore (son of the earlier governor) their new governor in place of the Proprietors' appointee Robert Johnson.

1720 The estimated population of the colony, excluding tribal Indians, was 18,500, of whom nearly 12,000 were black slaves.

Colonel John ("Tuscarora Jack") Barnwell was sent to England to speak for those who were now in power.

February 12. An act, the text of which has been lost, created the system of courts which lasted until the eve of the Revolution.

August 11. The Privy Council in England assumed responsibility for the government of South Carolina and appointed Francis Nicholson as the first royal governor.

1721 Fort King George, constructed by Colonel Barnwell on the Altamaha River and garrisoned by the Independent Company, remained an outpost until it was abandoned in September 1727.

A new act empowered watchmen in Charleston to stop Negroes on sight. The statewide patrol system that remained in effect until the Civil War evolved from this legislation.

May. Francis Nicholson and Colonel Barnwell with an Independent Company of British troops arrived in Charles Town.

September 19. A new election law was passed which again divided the representation among the parishes. The law established a property qualification of a fifty-acre freehold or twenty shillings paid in taxes. This remained the basic election law for the remainder of the colonial period until the American Revolution.

September 20. The Assembly, at the recommendation of Governor Francis Nicholson, created the province's first county courts, thus establishing South Carolina's first courts outside of Charleston. They did not, however, last the decade.

1722 *March 10.* The parish of Prince George Winyah was carved out of St. James's Santee.

March 25. Easter Day services were held for the first time in the new St. Philip's Church.

May 3. Mark Catesby, the naturalist, landed in Charles Town. At the direction of Sir Hans Sloane, founder of the British Museum, Catesby explored the backcountry and the Bahamas before returning to England in 1726. He published *The Natural History of Carolina, Florida, and the Bahama Islands* in two volumes (1731, 1743).

June 23. A law to incorporate the town and rename it Charles City and Port was passed this date, but it was disallowed in England.

1724 *February 24.* Henry Laurens was born.

1725 *December 14.* The Commons House of Assembly asserted its sole right to originate money bills and that the Council could only approve or reject such legislation.

1726 *June 26.* After a brief flurry of interest by the Proprietors in reestablishing their control of South Carolina, the Privy Council concluded the province should remain under royal control.

1727 *June.* The followers of the second Landgrave Thomas Smith, the leader of the anti-tax association in the northern parishes, marched on Charles Town.

1728 *February.* Colonel John Palmer led an attack upon the Yemassee settlements near St. Augustine.

1729 Georgetown was laid out on the banks of the Sampit River by William Swinton for Elisha Screven.

September 29. On this date the Lords Proprietors, with the exception of Lord Granville, formally surrendered their title and interest in Carolina for £2,500 sterling each.

November 30. The growing presence of the Scots in Charles Town was marked by the organization of the St. Andrew's Society.

1730 The estimated population of the colony, excluding tribal Indians, was 30,000, of whom approximately two-thirds were black slaves.

August. The first slave conspiracy in British South Carolina was detected and the ringleaders were immediately executed.

September 7. A treaty of friendship was signed in London between King George II and six Cherokee chiefs whom Sir Alexander Cuming had escorted to London. They had sailed from Charles Town on May 4 and returned with the new royal governor on December 15.

September 29. After this date Parliament permitted vessels with licenses obtained in England to carry rice directly to European ports south of Cape Finisterre, Spain.

November 23. William Moultrie was born.

December 15. Robert Johnson, the son of Sir Nathaniel Johnson and former governor under the Proprietors, arrived in Charles Town to assume the governorship of the new royal colony.

1731 *August 20.* A law establishing the royal quitrents put landholding on a secure and permanent basis. Registration of quitrents provided a permanent record of landholding.

August 20. A law stabilized the South Carolina paper currency on a ratio of seven to one with sterling. This exchange rate varied only slightly until the Revolution.

November 4. A printing press had been established by this date inasmuch as the first known South Carolina imprint, a proclamation of Governor Johnson, was issued on this day.

1732   Jean Pierre Purry, a Swiss promoter, obtained 12,000 acres on the Savannah River and helped to transport over 600 immigrants to Purrysburg.

Francis Marion was born; the exact date and place is unknown, but probably in Berkeley County.

January 8. The first South Carolina newspaper, the *South-Carolina Gazette,* was published by Thomas Whitmarsh in Charles Town.

1733   *January 13.* James Oglethorpe arrived in Charles Town with the first settlers for Georgia.

February 12. The town of Savannah, Georgia, was laid out on Yamacraw Bluff on the Savannah River.

April 23. The St. George's Society was founded in honor of the patron saint of England.

1734   *April 9.* The parish of St. John's Colleton was carved out of St. Paul's and the parish of Prince Frederick out of Prince George Winyah.

August 14. Thomas Sumter was born in Virginia.

1735   German Swiss immigrants began settlement in Orangeburg township.

Rhineland German immigrants began settling Saxe-Gotha township in modern Lexington County.

The governors of both Carolinas appointed a commission to survey the boundary between North Carolina and South Carolina.

January 24. Otway's tragedy, "The Orphan," was the initial performance of Charles Town's first theatrical season.

February 18. The first opera performed in America, "Flora, or Hob in the Well," was staged in Charles Town.

1736 Nicholas Trott had Lewis Timothy publish in Charles Town his two-volume work *The Laws of the Province of South Carolina.*

February 3. The Friendly Society for the Mutual Insuring of Houses against Fire was organized in Charles Town (the first fire insurance company in America).

February 12. The Dock Street Theatre opened with a performance of "The Recruiting Officer."

July 31. John Wesley made his first visit to Charles Town. He visited the city again April 14–23 and December 13–24, 1737. He sailed for England from Charles Town on December 24, 1737.

1737 The Boundary Commission completed the survey to define the boundary between North Carolina and South Carolina, which corresponded roughly to the modern boundary.

Welsh Baptists from Newcastle, Pennsylvania, settled in the Pee Dee region in what became known as the "Welsh Tract."

April. Dr. John Lining began his meteorological observations and notations.

1738 Inoculation for smallpox was first used in Charles Town during an epidemic after the disease had been brought to the city aboard a slave ship from Africa.

John Drayton bought the land on which he very soon built Drayton Hall, a sign of growing affluence in Carolina.

April 27, 28. A great fire occurred in Charles Town.

1739 *January.* By the Convention of El Pardo, England and Spain agreed that the land between the Altamaha and St. John's rivers should remain unsettled.

June 9. "A Prospect of Charlestown," an engraving based on Bishop Roberts' watercolor, was printed in London.

September. John Rutledge was born. His mother was only fifteen at the time of his birth.

September 9. Slaves from the Stono River plantations marched off toward St. Augustine, having heard that the Spaniards promised freedom. Forty blacks and twenty whites died in the insurrection.

September 19. Andrew Pickens was born in Pennsylvania.

October 23. The War of Jenkins' Ear began.

December 29. Charles Town printer Lewis Timothy died and his wife Ann continued publishing the *South-Carolina Gazette.* She was America's first female printer.

1740 The estimated population of the colony, excluding tribal Indians, was 60,000, of whom about two-thirds were black slaves.

April 5. After the Stono Rebellion the slave trade was greatly reduced by placing prohibitive taxes on the sale of recently imported slaves. The rate rose as high as £100 currency.

May 3. War against Spain was proclaimed in Charles Town with the usual ceremonies.

May 10. The basic law for regulating the life and activities of Negro slaves was passed. This slave code endured with little change until the Civil War.

June 12. The forces of General James Oglethorpe and the British navy besieged St. Augustine.

July 5. General Oglethorpe ordered the retreat.

July 15. An ecclesiastical court held in St. Philip's Church accused George Whitefield of conducting public services that did not follow the authorized forms of the Church of England Book of Common Prayer (Whitefield preached in Charleston several times in 1740 and 1741). This trial was the beginning of a process that led to Whitefield's expulsion from the Church of England and the eventual creation of the Methodist Church.

November 18. One of the most devastating of all

Charles Town fires destroyed half the buildings in the town and bankrupted the Friendly Society for the Mutual Insuring of Houses.

1741 Henry Middleton, by his marriage to Mary Williams, obtained the plantation he would develop into Middleton Place.

Spring. Patrick Tailfer, Hugh Anderson, and David Douglas published in Charles Town *A True and Historical Narrative* which placed the blame upon Oglethorpe for the failure of the 1740 expedition against St. Augustine.

1742 The Reverend Heinrich Melchior Muhlenberg visited Charles Town on his way from Ebenezer, Georgia, to Philadelphia and assisted in the establishment of the Lutheran Church in South Carolina.

July 7. The British defeated the Spaniards in the battle of Bloody Marsh on St. Simon's Island.

1743 *May 27.* Thomas Frankland, captain of HMS *Rose,* married Sarah Rhett, the granddaughter of Colonel William Rhett.

September 12. The Reverend Alexander Garden (d. 1773) opened a school for blacks in Charles Town. The purpose was to train them "in the principles of Christianity and the fundamentals of education, to serve as schoolmasters to their people."

December 17. James Glen arrived in Charles Town to assume the governorship. His term (until June 1, 1756) proved to be the longest of any South Carolina colonial governor.

1744 Eliza Lucas Pinckney proved that indigo could be grown in South Carolina, the equal of that grown by the French and Spaniards in the West Indies.

March. King George's War began in Europe as the War of Austrian Succession.

May 27. Eliza Lucas became the second wife of Charles Pinckney (d. 1758), the former speaker of the Commons House of Assembly.

July 23. War was proclaimed in Charles Town against France. Many Spanish and French ships were captured by the British Navy in the ensuing months and brought as prizes to Charles Town.

December. The 400-ton French ship *Conception,* captured off Cuba (with a cargo that included much gold and silver) by HMS *Rose* under Captain Thomas Frankland, reached Charles Town as a prize of war, estimated to be worth £80,000 sterling (including cargo).

1745 *May 25.* Prince William parish was carved out of St. Helena's.

1746 *February 25.* Charles Cotesworth Pinckney was born.

1747 *February 17.* The township of Purrysburg and adjacent parts were erected into the parish of St. Peter.

1748 The English Parliament granted a six-pence-per-pound bounty to the producers of Carolina indigo.

February 17, 18. The temperature fell to ten degrees Fahrenheit, the coldest day in Charles Town in the eighteenth century. The intense cold killed the orange trees which many believed could grow in Carolina.

June 21. The Assembly lowered the maximum legal interest on debts from 10 to 8 percent.

December 28. The Charles Town Library Society was organized on this date; it was incorporated by the province on May 8, 1754.

1749 The congregation Beth Elohim was organized in Charles Town by those who had come from the Spanish and Portuguese Jewish communities of London as well as the West Indies.

June 12. The peace signed at Aix-la-Chapelle in October 1748, which ended the War of Austrian Succession, was proclaimed in Charles Town.

November 23. Edward Rutledge was born.

1750 The estimated population of the colony, excluding tribal Indians, was 65,000, of whom about two-thirds were black slaves.

October 23. Thomas Pinckney was born.

1751 *May 17.* The South Carolina Society was incorporated.

June 14. The parish of St. Philip's was divided; the part below Broad Street became the parish of St. Michael's.

1752 *June 23.* The Trustees of Georgia signed the indenture by which Georgia became a royal colony with a governmental structure similar to that of South Carolina.

September 15, 30. Two great hurricanes hit Charles Town in succession.

1753 Fort Prince George was built at Keowee.

Construction of the State House was begun at the northwest corner of Broad and Meeting streets. It was occupied by 1756. At the same time construction of St. Michael's Church began on the southeast corner.

July 6. James Crokatt's announcement that he desired to retire as South Carolina's colonial agent resulted in a struggle between the Assembly and the Council over the selection of a successor. The Council lost both power and prestige in the contest.

October 27. In London Peter Leigh was appointed chief justice of South Carolina to supercede Charles Pinckney (d. 1758) who held a temporary appointment to that position.

1754 The congregation at Dorchester on the Ashley River moved to Midway, Georgia.

May 11. The parish of St. Stephen was carved out of St. James's Santee.

July 3. Lieutenant Peter Mercier of the Independent Company was killed in the Virginia backcountry at Great Meadows while serving under the command of George Washington.

1755 More than 1,000 Acadians arrived from Nova Scotia. They failed to assimilate and by 1760 barely 200 remained in the province.

1756 The province purchased in London the mace which is still used by the legislature.

May 17. King George II declared war on France. Thus formally began the Great War for the Empire (the French and Indian War).

June 1. William Henry Lyttelton arrived to assume the governorship.

September 2. The declaration of war against France was proclaimed in Charles Town.

October. The construction of Fort Loudoun on the Little Tennessee River began.

November 29. Governor Lyttelton suspended William Wragg from the Royal Council.

1757 *May 21.* The Winyah Indigo Society of Georgetown was incorporated.

May 21. The parish of St. Mark was carved out of Prince Frederick.

July. Fort Loudoun was completed.

October 26. Charles Pinckney (d. 1824), first cousin once removed of Charles Cotesworth and Thomas Pinckney, was born.

1758 *July 13.* Charles Pinckney, the father of Charles Cotesworth and Thomas Pinckney, died.

1759 *November–December.* Governor Lyttelton's expedition against the Cherokees ended with a treaty hastily drawn on December 26.

1760 The estimated population of the colony, excluding tribal Indians, was 84,000, of whom about 52,000 were black slaves.

January 12. The soldiers returning to Charles Town from the Cherokee campaign brought back smallpox and a virulent epidemic ensued.

February 1. The mother of Patrick Calhoun was one of twenty-three people slain by the Cherokee Indians near Long Canes Creek.

February 16. Cherokee hostages being held at Fort Prince George were massacred by the soldiers.

March 13. John Bartram, America's outstanding botanist, arrived at Charles Town to visit Dr. Alexander Garden (d. 1791) and study southern plants during his first trip to South Carolina.

April 1. Colonel Archibald Montgomery arrived in Charles Town from the north with 1,200 Highland troops and soon marched against the Cherokees.

June 27. After being ambushed, Montgomery's force retreated to Charles Town.

August 8. The besieged garrison at Fort Loudoun was starved into surrendering. On the next day the Cherokees massacred the garrison but Attakullakulla ("The Little Carpenter") saved the life of Captain John Stuart.

August. Montgomery reached Charles Town and sailed for the North with most of his troops.

1761 *February 1.* Divine service was performed for the first time in St. Michael's Church.

March 20. British troops from New York, accompanied by the South Carolina Provincial Regiment led by Thomas Middleton, marched under the command of Lieutenant Colonel James Grant from Charles Town against the Cherokees.

June 10. Grant broke the power of the Cherokees at the battle of Etchohih near their town of Estatoe which he destroyed the next day.

September 23. A treaty was drawn up at Ashley Ferry Town between the Cherokees and Lieutenant Governor William Bull.

October–November. Grant and his force returned to Charles Town.

December. Middleton accused Grant of failure to consult him during the successful campaign. The two fought a duel in which neither was injured, but the dispute dramatized the jealousies that had arisen between the provincial and the royal officers.

December 17. The first of Christopher Gadsden's "Philopatrios" pamphlets attacking Colonel Grant was printed in the *South-Carolina Gazette.* The second was published in May 1762. Henry Laurens, who defended Grant, circulated his pamphlet privately under the pseudonym "Philolethes."

December 22. Thomas Boone arrived to assume the governorship.

1762 The St. Cecilia Society, a musical organization, was formed in Charles Town.

January 12. John Stuart was appointed British Superintendent of Indian Affairs in the South. The commission, dated January 5, did not reach him until May 1762.

April 10. War against Spain was proclaimed in Charles Town.

June 5. Henry Laurens bought Mepkin plantation on the Western Branch of the Cooper River. Laurens, like many other merchants, invested his wartime profits in land.

September 13. Governor Boone refused to administer the state oaths to Christopher Gadsden upon his election to the Assembly from St. Paul's parish, a hotbed of dissent. This raised a constitutional crisis.

December 16. The Assembly resolved to do no further business with the governor until he should recognize the rights and privileges of members of the Commons House of Assembly. Little legislative business was transacted until after Boone left the province in May 1764.

1763 *February 10.* The Treaty of Paris ended the Great War for the Empire.

April 17. Lord William Campbell, the fourth son of the Duke of Argyle, married a South Carolina heiress, Sarah Izard. Lord William was captain of HMS *Nightingale* which was stationed on the Carolina coast. Later appointed governor, Campbell returned to South Carolina on June 18, 1775.

May. Governor Boone and the Royal Council granted lands to Carolinians south of the Altamaha River.

August 27. The peace signed at Paris on February 10 was proclaimed in Charles Town.

November 10. The Treaty of Augusta was signed by the governors of Georgia, South Carolina, North Carolina, and Virginia, and by the chiefs of the Cherokees, Creeks, Chickasaws, Choctaws, and Catawbas. John Stuart as Superintendent of Indian Affairs for the Southern District presided over the conference. This treaty set aside a ten-square-mile reservation for the Catawbas.

1764 *May 11.* Governor Boone set sail for England accompanied by the wife of Samuel Peronneau.

July 29. Packetboat service was established between Falmouth, England, and Charles Town, with the *Grenville Packet* arriving at Charles Town on this date.

III. REVOLUTION
(1765–1790)

By 1765 the English settlement originally called *Charles Town* had gotten into the habit of spelling its name as one word, *Charlestown*, and no doubt many of its citizens were already pronouncing it as *Charleston*, although that did not become its official name until 1783, after the British had been expelled.

No other colony had such close ties with England, for the great merchants of Charlestown owed much of their wealth to trade with, or through, London, a city they frequently visited. Thus, in their first instincts, most South Carolinians were loyal to the British crown. But the misjudgment of George III's government in greatly increasing taxes that might have crippled the colony's economy and the insensitivity of the British governors in recognizing the needs and aspirations of the people, as in the case in 1772 of trying to move the capital from Charlestown to Beaufort, brought South Carolina into the Revolution. Once the fighting began and English troops invaded the colony, British commanders mistreated the civilians as well as the prisoners of war and those who had given their paroles. Consequently the Carolinians were more determined than ever to continue the fight. Although British troops were able to occupy Charlestown from May 12, 1780, to December 14, 1782, the brilliant guerilla campaigns of Francis Marion (the "Swamp Fox") and Thomas Sumter (the "Gamecock") tied up British resources in futile attempts to control the countryside and were a decisive factor in the eventual defeat of the British.

After the British troops evacuated Charlestown, South Carolina was at last an independent state. South Carolina statesmen such as John Rutledge, Charles Cotesworth Pinckney, Charles Pinckney, Pierce Butler,

William Loughton Smith, Robert Goodloe Harper, and David Ramsay played major roles in the creation of the U.S. Constitution and the development of the early republic, these leaders generally taking the Federalist side. Since the 1740s there had been a steady immigration from Pennsylvania and Virginia of frontier farmers into the backcountry of the state, where they grew tobacco for export and provision crops for the lowcountry slaves. By the end of the Revolutionary period Charleston was forced to recognize them as a very important element in the state government. Their leaders, Wade Hampton, Andrew Pickens, Nathaniel Pendleton, and Robert Anderson, generally took the Republican side. When Pierce Butler and Charles Pinckney took up backcountry causes, the movement was successful in transferring the capital from Charleston to Columbia, and in 1790 remaking the state constitution to meet backcountry requests for greater representation and share in state offices.

1765 *March 22.* In England, Parliament passed the Stamp Act.

October 7–25. John Rutledge, Christopher Gadsden, and Thomas Lynch represented South Carolina at the Stamp Act Congress which was held in New York.

October 18. The stamped paper arrived in Charlestown harbor.

October 23. A masked and armed mob searched the home of Henry Laurens for stamped paper.

October 28. The stamp agents for South Carolina were coerced by a large crowd at Charlestown to promise not to issue any stamps until Parliament reviewed the act.

November 1. The Stamp Act went into effect. Clearances for ships could not be issued and courts could not conduct their business without stamped paper. The port was at a standstill.

November 29. The Commons House of Assembly by an almost unanimous vote (only William Wragg objected) adopted the report of Gadsden's committee which set forth the rights and duties of English subjects.

Christmas. There was threat of a slave insurrection.

1766 *January 1.* On this date the slave trade was effectively cut off for a period of three years by the act which had been passed on August 25, 1764, to impose a £100 tax on each slave imported.

January 15. The German Friendly Society was organized at the home of Michael Kalteisen.

March 18. Parliament repealed the Stamp Act and passed the Declaratory Act.

May 3. News of the repeal of the Stamp Act reached Charlestown. A great celebration was held that evening.

June 12. Lord Charles Greville Montagu arrived in Charlestown to assume the governorship.

September 12. The Reverend Charles Woodmason left Charlestown for the backcountry where he became an advocate for the Regulators.

December. Fort Charlotte was completed on the north bank of the Savannah River upstream from old Fort Moore.

1767 Construction of the Exchange began in Charlestown at the east end of Broad Street under the direction of Peter and John Adam Horlbeck. Completed in 1772 and still standing, it is the most historic building in the state.

March 15. Andrew Jackson was born in the Waxhaw area of South Carolina.

May. The sloop *Active* was seized by Captain James Hawker of HMS *Sardoine.* Thus began a major contest between the British authorities and the Carolina merchants.

May 23. The parish of St. Luke was carved out of St. Helena's and the parish of All Saints out of Prince George Winyah. Although these acts were disallowed and the new parishes dissolved in 1770, the parish of All Saints was recreated on March 16, 1778, and the parish of St. Luke on February 29, 1788.

June. The sloops *Wambaw* and *Broughton Island Packet,* owned by Henry Laurens, were seized by the British authorities.

September. The collector of the customs, Daniel Moore, was run out of town.

October 6. The governor issued a proclamation ordering those who led the Regulator movement in the backcountry to cease and desist.

November 7. The Regulators made a statement of their grievances.

1768 *April 12.* The governor signed the Circuit Court Act which was designed to meet the grievances of the backcountry men who desired courts and jails. This law was disallowed in England because the royal government insisted that the judges should sit at the pleasure of the Crown.

April 12. The parish of St. Matthew was established in Berkeley County and that of St. David in Craven County.

June. A Plan of Regulation was adopted by a gathering of Regulators at the Congarees.

June. The case against Henry Laurens' ship *Ann* was a *cause* célèbre.

July 25. There was a skirmish between the Regulators and the Provincial authorities at Mars Bluff on the Pee Dee River.

August 3. The governor issued a proclamation calling for the suppression of the Regulator movement.

August 6. The governor by proclamation offered pardon to the Regulators who would drop their opposition to constituted authority.

October 4–5. At this crucial election the power of the backcountry was first felt when many voters came down from the interior to vote at the parish churches.

November 19. Twenty-six members of the Assembly voted unanimously to consider the Massachusetts Circular Letter and thereby brought on the dissolution of the Assembly by the royal governor. "Twenty-six" became a sacred number in Carolina's Revolutionary iconography.

1769 *March 25.* A truce was arranged between the Regulators and the Moderators which brought the Regulation to an end.

July 22. A committee of thirteen merchants, thirteen planters, and thirteen mechanics was established to enforce the nonimportation agreements which were South Carolina's protest against the Townshend duties passed by the English Parliament in 1767.

July 29. A second Circuit Court Act was passed. The legislation created seven judicial districts— Charlestown was one district; Beaufort, Orangeburg, and Ninety Six made up the Southern circuit; Georgetown, Cheraw, and Camden comprised the Northern Circuit. This law was allowed to stand by the British authorities because the judges would now serve at the pleasure of the Crown. By the direction of this law, courts and jails were constructed in the six outlying districts by 1772.

August 23. The Fellowship Society was incorporated.

December 8. The Assembly voted to send £1,500 sterling to support the cause of John Wilkes in England.

1770 The estimated population of the province, excluding tribal Indians, was 130,000, of whom about 80,000 were black slaves.

April 14. When George III heard of the gift to Wilkes, he ordered his government to send out an Additional Instruction which denied the authority of the Assembly to appropriate funds for such a purpose and reaffirmed the coordinate authority of the Royal Council in the colony to amend and to pass money bills. An impasse thereupon ensued which kept the Assembly from doing any real business for the remainder of the colonial period.

July 5. The statue of William Pitt, designed by Joseph Wilton, which had been commissioned to honor South Carolina's English friend after the repeal of the Stamp Act, was erected in the crossing of Broad and Meeting streets.

December 13. South Carolina broke through the nonimportation agreements, thereby opening up the port of Charlestown to commerce once again.

1771 *March 20.* An inspection system for tobacco was established at public warehouses on the principal rivers and at the ports. This was a sign that the backcountry had been filling up and had found a commercial crop.

October 31. The Regulators were pardoned.

1772 *October 8–10.* Governor Lord Charles Montagu called the Assembly to meet in Beaufort hoping thereby to control that body once it was removed from the influence of the Charlestown patriots.

November. The backcountry courts began to function. The judges held court on November 5 at Camden and Orangeburg, on November 16 at Cheraw and Ninety Six, on November 25 at Georgetown, and on November 30 at Beaufort.

1773 William Wofford established the first iron works in South Carolina at Lawson's Fork of the Pacolet River.

January. A committee of the Charlestown Library Society was appointed to consider establishing a museum. This was the origin of the Charlestown Museum. In June Lieutenant Governor William Bull II, president of the Library Society, announced the formation of a special committee for collecting materials.

May 10. The Tea Act became law.

December 9. The Charlestown Chamber of Commerce was organized.

December 22. The tea that had been brought to Charlestown under the Tea Act was unloaded and stored in the basement of the recently-built Exchange.

1774 *July 6–8.* A General Meeting of the people in Charlestown elected Christopher Gadsden, Thomas Lynch, Henry Middleton, Edward Rutledge, and John Rutledge the province's delegates to the First Continental Congress. This meeting also selected a General Committee, headed by Charles Pinckney (d. 1782), to direct the interests of South Carolina during the turmoil.

October 22–26. Henry Middleton served as the second president of the Continental Congress.

December 1. On this date the continental nonimportation agreement went into effect.

1775 *January 11–17.* The first session of the First Provincial Congress met in Charlestown and selected

Charles Pinckney (d. 1782) president. The backcountry had 46 representatives in this extralegal legislative body of 184 delegates.

April 21. The public powder and arms in the magazines at Hobcaw, on Charlestown Neck, and at the State House were seized.

May. A letter from Arthur Lee in London to Henry Laurens conveyed a rumor that the British intended to incite both slaves and Indians against the patriots. This sensational rumor increased opposition to the royal government.

May 8. The news of the fighting at Lexington and Concord reached Charlestown.

June 1–22. The second session of the First Provincial Congress met and selected Henry Laurens president.

June 3. The members of the Provincial Congress voted unanimously to adopt the Association and called upon all Carolinians to sign it. They pledged to unite themselves in the defense of their state.

June 14. The Provincial Congress by its own authority ordered the printing of £1 million currency.

June 14. A Council of Safety was elected by the Provincial Congress with Henry Laurens selected president of the body.

June 18. The last of the royal governors, Lord William Campbell, arrived in Charlestown.

July 12. South Carolina patriots captured Fort Charlotte on the Savannah River.

August 18. The patriots in Charlestown "hanged and burned" the free black pilot Thomas Jeremiah. "Jerry" was accused of instigating an insurrection and threatening to assist the Royal Navy when they came to punish the wayward Carolinians.

August–September. William Henry Drayton, the Reverend Oliver Hart, and the Reverend William Tennent toured the backcountry to explain the patriot position.

September 10. On this date the continental nonexportation agreement went into effect. Rice, however, had been excepted from that agreement.

September 15. Lord William Campbell fled from his home on Meeting Street to HMS *Tamar* anchored in Charlestown harbor. He took with him the Great Seal of the Royal Province.

November 1–29. The first session of the Second Provincial Congress met and selected William Henry Drayton president.

November 11, 12. In the first South Carolina engagement of the Revolution, HMS *Tamar* and HMS *Cherokee* fired upon the schooner *Defence* which was trying to sink four hulks to block Hog Island channel.

November 19–21. Major Andrew Williamson was attacked by Tories at Ninety Six. In this second engagement of the Revolution in South Carolina the first blood was shed.

December. Colonel Richard Richardson came to the aid of Williamson and pacified the backcountry. Because of the weather this became known as the Snow Campaign.

1776 *February 1–March 26.* The second session of the Second Provincial Congress met.

February 8. Christopher Gadsden returned from Philadelphia carrying the first copies of Thomas Paine's *Common Sense* to South Carolina.

February 27. North Carolina patriots defeated Loyalists at the battle of Moore's Creek Bridge.

March 26. South Carolina adopted its first state constitution which had been drawn up by the Provincial Congress. John Rutledge was elected the first president and Henry Laurens the first vice president.

April 2. President Rutledge was authorized to design a Great Seal for the state.

April 11. South Carolina established its own vice admiralty court.

April 23. Chief Justice William Henry Drayton delivered an eloquent and inflammatory charge to the Charlestown grand jury upon the opening of South Carolina courts under the new constitution.

June 1. British troops 2,500 strong landed on Long Island (Isle of Palms).

June 28. At the battle of Fort Moultrie, William Moultrie's band of patriots, in their newly constructed palmetto log fort, repulsed the attempt of Sir Peter Parker to sail the British fleet into

Charlestown harbor (the palmetto tree later became a state symbol). William Thompson's upcountrymen prevented Sir Henry Clinton's troops from crossing Breach Inlet from Long Island to Sullivan's Island. And in the midst of the bombardment of Fort Moultrie Sergeant Jasper rescued the flag.

July 2. The South Carolina delegation to the Continental Congress voted in favor of American Independence.

July 15–October 11. Andrew Williamson crushed the Cherokees.

August 2. Arthur Middleton, Edward Rutledge, Thomas Lynch, Jr., and Thomas Heyward, Jr., signed the Declaration of Independence in Philadelphia.

August 5. The news of the adoption of the Declaration of Independence reached Charlestown.

October 8. A Board of Naval Commissioners was established with Edward Blake as the first commissioner.

1777 *January 23.* William Henry Drayton, at the direction of the South Carolina Assembly, presented a plan to the Georgia Convention under which South Carolina would annex its less populous neighbor. Georgia rejected the proposal the following day.

February 13. An oath of abjuration of loyalty to King George III and of allegiance to the new state was demanded of each white male citizen. Those who would not take such an oath were banished.

May 20. By the Treaty of DeWitt's Corner between the patriots and the Cherokees, South Carolina obtained most of present-day Greenville, Pickens, Oconee, and Anderson counties. Settlers immediately flocked to this backcountry area.

May 22. The state seal, which had been authorized on April 2, 1776, was used for the first time by President John Rutledge.

June 13. The Marquis de Lafayette and the Baron de Kalb stepped ashore on North Island and made their way to the home of Benjamin Huger, having come from France to join the American cause.

June 28. First Palmetto Day.

November 1. Henry Laurens was elected president of the Continental Congress. He served until December 9, 1778.

1778 *January 15.* A great Charlestown fire destroyed, among other things, the library and the museum.

March 6. Rawlins Lowndes was elected president of the state upon the resignation of John Rutledge, who could not accept the new constitution.

March 7. The Continental frigate *Randolph* and four vessels of the South Carolina Navy fought an engagement with HMS *Yarmouth* east of Barbados. The *Randolph* exploded and the South Carolina Navy was dispersed.

March 11. Alexander Gillon, an ambitious Dutch merchant who had settled in Charlestown, was appointed commodore of the South Carolina Navy.

March 16. Orange parish was cut off from St. Matthew's.

March 19. South Carolina adopted its second state constitution, which disestablished the Church of England.

March 28. A law passed under the new constitution demanded an assurance of fidelity to the state.

July 9. Henry Laurens, William Henry Drayton, John Mathews, Richard Hutson, and Thomas Heyward, Jr., signed the Articles of Confederation, thereby signifying South Carolina's acceptance of that document.

November. The Southern campaign against Georgia and the Carolinas began with the arrival on the Georgia coast of Lieutenant Colonel Archibald Campbell with British troops from the northward.

December 29. Campbell drove General Robert Howe and the patriots out of Savannah.

1779 *January 9.* John Rutledge was elected the state's first governor.

February 3. The British attempted an amphibious landing at Port Royal Island but were driven off by Continental troops commanded by General William Moultrie and South Carolina militia led by Brigadier General Stephen Bull. Two signers of the Declaration of Independence, Thomas Heyward, Jr., and Edward Rutledge, served as captains of South Carolina companies in the battle.

February 14. At the battle of Kettle Creek in Georgia Andrew Pickens defeated a larger Loyalist force from North Carolina.

June 20. General William Moultrie attacked Augustine Prevost who had retreated from the walls of Charlestown to the ferry at Stono River.

September 1. The arrival of the Comte d'Estaing with a French fleet off Tybee Island made it possible for the patriots to besiege Savannah.

October 9. A major assault on the defenses of Savannah failed to carry the city. Sergeant Jasper and the Comte Pulaski died in the attack.

1780 The estimated population of the state was 180,000, of whom about 97,000 were black slaves.

February 3. Extraordinary powers were vested in Governor John Rutledge for a period to end ten days after the next meeting of the legislature. Thus the governor became "Dictator" Rutledge.

February 11. Sir Henry Clinton disembarked his army on Johns Island.

March 27. Two great cavalry leaders, Colonel Banastre Tarleton and Colonel William Washington, clashed near Rantowle's Bridge over the Stono River.

March 29. The British invested Charlestown— Clinton by land, the ships of Marriot Arbuthnot by sea.

April 14. Colonel Tarleton and Major Patrick Ferguson dispersed the patriot forces commanded by General Isaac Huger at Moncks Corner and thereby cut off the escape route from Charlestown for Benjamin Lincoln's forces.

May 6. Fort Moultrie fell to the British.

May 9–12. The bombardment of Charlestown.

May 12. General Lincoln surrendered Charlestown, with over 5,000 troops and 50,000 pounds of gunpower, to General Clinton.

May 29. Tarleton caught the fleeing Abraham Buford and his Virginians at the Waxhaws and cut them down.

May 30. Commodore Gillon and the Chevalier de Luxembourg signed a contract in France in which the frigate *Indien* was turned over to Gillon for a term of three years. Gillon renamed the *Indien* the *South Carolina*.

June 3. Clinton demanded the paroles of the leading South Carolinians.

June 5. The loyal citizens of Charlestown presented addresses of congratulation to Clinton and Arbuthnot. Those who signed had their estates confiscated by the patriot legislature when it met at Jacksonborough in January–February 1782.

June 8. Clinton sailed for New York leaving General Charles Lord Cornwallis in command at Charlestown.

June 18. Loyalist Christian Huck destroyed William Hill's Iron Works in the New Acquisition District.

July 12. Huck was killed and his Loyalist force defeated at Williamson's Plantation in a bloody action, typical of the fighting in the South Carolina backcountry.

August 6. Thomas Sumter, trying to organize resistance in the backcountry, attacked the Loyalists at Hanging Rock.

August 15, 16. General Charles Lord Cornwallis defeated Horatio Gates at the battle of Camden, where Baron de Kalb lost his life.

August 18. Tarleton surprised Sumter at Fishing Creek.

August 18. Musgrove's Mill was a dress rehearsal for King's Mountain.

August 27. On this evening twenty-nine prominent Charlestonians including Christopher Gadsden were taken into custody. They and others were later shipped off to St. Augustine.

September 19. The loyal citizens of Charlestown presented Cornwallis with an address of congratulations for his victory at Camden. Those who participated had their estates confiscated by the patriot legislature when it met at Jacksonborough in January–February 1782.

September 29. Francis Marion struck at the loyal militia led by John Coming Ball at Black Mingo Creek Bridge.

October 6. Henry Laurens was shut up in the Tower of London. On September 3, while on a mission from Congress to Holland to seek a loan, he had been taken on the high seas off Newfoundland and sent to London. He remained in the Tower until December 31, 1781, at which time he was exchanged for Lord Cornwallis.

October 7. The mountain men defeated the loyal militia raised by Major Patrick Ferguson at the battle of King's Mountain, one of the decisive battles of the Revolution.

November 9. Sumter repulsed the British cavalry at Fishdam Ford and barely escaped a small party the British sent to kill him.

November 20. At Blackstock's plantation in a bend of the Tyger River, Sumter fought Tarleton to a standoff.

December 2. General Nathanael Greene arrived at Charlotte, North Carolina, to take command of the Southern Continental Army.

1781 *January 17.* Daniel Morgan defeated Tarleton at the battle of Cowpens.

January 25. Francis Marion with the assistance of Light Horse Harry Lee captured the British commander at Georgetown.

February 14. Greene crossed the Dan River to safety in Virginia after leading Cornwallis in a merry chase through North Carolina.

March 15. Greene faced Cornwallis at the battle of Guilford Courthouse.

April 23. Lee and Marion, again cooperating, forced the surrender of Fort Watson on the Santee

River after Hezekiah Maham built a wooden tower which permitted the patriots to rake the interior of the fort with gunfire.

April 25. Colonel Francis Lord Rawdon opposed Greene at Hobkirk's Hill just north of Camden.

May 8–12. The siege of Fort Motte concluded when Rebecca Motte urged the patriots to shoot flaming arrows into her home, which the British were using as a fort.

May 11. Orangeburg surrendered to Sumter.

May 15. Fort Granby on the Congaree surrendered to Lee.

May 22–June 19. Ninety Six, the last of the British garrisons in the upcountry, was besieged by Greene until Lord Rawdon raised the siege after he had received reinforcements in Charlestown.

August 4. The British executed Isaac Hayne in Charlestown.

September 8. The battle of Eutaw Springs, the bloodiest encounter in the Southern Campaign, was the last major engagement in the state.

November 8. After retiring to the High Hills of the Santee after the battle of Eutaw Springs, Greene once again invaded the lowcountry and established his army at Round O in Colleton County.

December. The British abandoned Dorchester, their post on the Ashley River, which has remained a ruin ever since.

1782 *January 8–February 26.* The South Carolina legislature under the protection of Greene's army met at Jacksonborough on the Edisto River to restore civil government to the state.

January 31. John Mathews was elected governor after Gadsden refused the honor.

February 26. The estates of many Loyalists were confiscated.

February 26. South Carolina ratified an amendment to the Articles of Confederation which would have permitted the Continental Congress to levy a 5 percent ad valorem import duty.

March 18. John C. Calhoun was born.

August 27. John Laurens was killed at Combahee Bluff, in one of the last minor engagements of the Revolution, by a British force in search of supplies for the besieged garrison of Charlestown.

September 6. A British fleet sailed into Charlestown harbor to evacuate the British force stationed there.

November 14. Dills Bluff (James Island) was the last Revolutionary battle in the state.

November 30. In Paris, Henry Laurens, along with Benjamin Franklin, John Adams, and John Jay, signed the preliminary treaty of peace.

December 14. Charlestown was evacuated by the British forces, who took away over 3,000 Loyalists and 5,000 slaves.

1783 David Ramsay wrote that by this year Gideon Du-Pont had perfected the tidal culture of rice. It is impossible to pin to one date such a fundamental change in the cultivation of rice, the state's leading staple. Yet by the 1780s rice was being grown in the river swamps where the fluctuation of the tides could be used to flood and drain the fields.

August 13. Charleston was incorporated as a city in a move designed to restore order to a community still wracked by turbulence. The name of the city was henceforth "Charleston."

August 29. General William Moultrie called the Continental officers to meet at the City Tavern, northeast corner of Church and Broad streets, to form the South Carolina chapter of the Cincinnati.

September 23. The Peace of Paris ended the war of the American Revolution.

October 6. The members of the Cincinnati signed the Institution of the Order of the Cincinnati.

1784 *March 26.* The manner in which an alien could become a citizen of the new state was described by law.

1785 Ann Donovan Timothy began to publish the *State Gazette of South-Carolina* and became "Printer to the State."

David Ramsay published in two volumes *The History of the Revolution of South-Carolina, from a British Province to an Independent State.*

March 19. The College of Charleston was incorporated. Students were accepted by 1790. An attempt to establish colleges at Winnsborough and Ninety Six at this time failed.

March 24. The County Court Act divided the state into counties and established a system of county courts. These courts were abolished in 1799. Abbeville, Laurens, Spartanburg, Newberry, Union, York, Chester, Fairfield, Lewisburg (Lexington), Richland, Lancaster, Chesterfield, Darlington, Marlboro, Barnwell, Williamsburg, and Winton (Edgefield) were included in the act.

August 4. The Chamber of Commerce was revived to help South Carolina seek new avenues of commerce.

August 24. The Agricultural Society of South Carolina was organized in order to search for new staples.

October 12. An issue of £100,000 in paper bills was authorized in order to spark the new economy.

1786 Greenville County was created from land acquired from the Cherokees during the American Revolution.

March 11. South Carolina ratified an amendment to the Articles of Confederation which would have given the Continental Congress the power to regulate commerce with foreign nations. Having ratified the amendment, South Carolina saw no reason to send a delegation to the Annapolis convention.

March 13. Charles Pinckney (d. 1824), a delegate to the Continental Congress, urged the legislature of New Jersey to contribute its assessment to support the government of the Confederation. In this speech Pinckney outlined needed changes in the central government, the seed of the Pinckney plan of 1787.

March 22. The Santee Canal Company was incorporated. A canal which linked the Santee and Cooper rivers was opened by 1799.

March 22. The legislature agreed to move the capital of the state to the upcountry. The new town would be called Columbia and would be situated near Friday's Ferry on the Congaree River on land two miles square, including the plain of the hill owned by Thomas and James Taylor.

May 3. Charles Pinckney (d. 1824) inaugurated an ambitious movement in the Congress to reorganize the government under the Articles of Confederation.

September 29. Scottish merchants in Charleston organized the South Carolina Golf Club. Until 1800 the game of golf was played on Harleston's Green in Charleston.

1787   Jonathan Lucas built the first tidal rice mill at John Bowman's Peach Island plantation on the Santee River.

John Gabriel Guignard laid out Columbia.

March 8. South Carolina agreed to cede its western lands to the Confederation.

March 28. The foreign slave trade was cut off for a period of three years. As this legislation was several times renewed, the slave trade was cut off until 1803.

May 29. Charles Pinckney (d. 1824) presented his plan to the constitutional convention in Philadelphia.

August 9. John Kean and Daniel Huger executed a deed of cession of South Carolina's western lands to the Confederation.

September 17. John Rutledge, Charles Cotesworth Pinckney, Charles Pinckney (d. 1824), and Pierce Butler signed the new Constitution of the United States.

1788 *January 19.* The legislature agreed to call a convention of the people to consider the ratification of the Constitution.

February 5. The State House in Charleston burned (construction of the new State House in Columbia had already begun).

May 12–23. The Ratification Convention met in Charleston.

May 23. South Carolina ratified the Constitution.

November 4. A law which permitted the payment of certain debts in five installments was passed. This type of law was void under the new U.S. Constitution which forbade the states from impairing the obligation of contracts.

George Washington was elected President. South Carolina cast seven electoral votes for him, six for John Rutledge, and one for John Hancock.

1789 David Ramsay published in two volumes *The History of the American Revolution*.

December 1. The records of the state were moved from Charleston to Columbia.

1790 **U.S. Census**

White	140,178
Slave	107,094
Free Black	1,801
Total	249,073

William Elliott first planted Sea Island cotton at the northwest point of Hilton Head Island.

January 4. The first session of the legislature to be held in Columbia opened.

January 18–19. South Carolina ratified the Bill of Rights (the first ten amendments of the U.S. Constitution).

May 10–June 3. A state constitutional convention met in Columbia to write the third state constitution. The first two constitutions had been written by the legislative branch.

June 3. The third state constitution was signed by the members of the convention, but it was not sent out to the people for ratification.

November 1. The Brown Fellowship Society was founded in Charleston.

IV. THE STATE AND THE UNION (1791–1859)

Except for the War of 1812 with Great Britain, South Carolina and the other states of the Union were isolated from such upheavals in Europe as the French Revolution (1789–1799). South Carolina shared the troubles, especially the fiscal troubles, of the young nation, but recovered a great deal of its prosperity as cotton exports boomed after 1800. While the industrial revolution was taking place in the Northern states, South Carolina, despite the presence of inventors and innovators (like Abraham Blanding, Robert Mills, and later James M. Legaré), despite the talent for management that the planters had long since developed, and despite the obvious opportunities for water-powered mills (a few of which were indeed started), remained a staple-exporting region, importing manufactured goods from England and the North. In this, and in the slave trade which continued intermittently until 1808 and at times even illegally until the middle of the nineteenth century, lay South Carolina's tragedy. Outside the Southern states, the civilized world came more and more to see slavery as an ugly anachronism. Proposals from the Northern manufacturing states to levy tariffs on manufactured imports jeopardized South Carolina's economic system and were brilliantly resisted by John C. Calhoun, who developed the first critique of the rapidly centralizing forces in the United States and the spiritual bankruptcy of industrial civilization.

In the 1820s many whites moved southwest to Alabama, Mississippi, Louisiana, and Texas, taking with them the system of exporting slave-cultivated cotton while adding sugar to the staple crops. South Carolina was at first in a lonely position, for no other Southern state owed so much wealth to slave labor. But gradually the skillful diplomacy of South Carolina's leaders, the emigration that resulted in like-minded communities in the west, the eagerness of industrialists in the middle Atlantic states to penalize foreign competitors with tariffs, and the steadily growing abhorrence of slavery among those who did not own slaves or feel indebted to slave-owners led to a coalition of Southern states behind the intellectual leadership of South Carolina.

It should be remembered, however, that a great many white South Carolinians never owned slaves, that a small minority of them opposed the perpetuation of slavery and moved north of the Ohio River, and that many opposed separation from the Union and from the modern way of life that it was coming to embody. Nevertheless, a Southern style of life that included fear as well as exploitation of the blacks united most white South Carolinians in defense of slavery.

It was intelligence, not cowardice, that prevented most black South Carolinians from openly rising in rebellion, for if a slave rebellion failed it would only harden the determination of the whites and if it succeeded where could the rebellious slaves settle safely, prosperously, and in large numbers?

During the period from American independence to the Civil War, many white South Carolinians enjoyed enough freedom and ease to allow the arts, especially architecture, to flourish. South Carolina College rapidly became an intellectual center that flourished unlike any the South had had before and hardly any seen since. But perhaps the most positive achievement of the age was the development of a characteristically Southern celebration of rural and agricultural values by such writers as William Grayson and William Gilmore Simms.

1791 The revolt of the slaves in Santo Domingo raised the specter of a slave rebellion in America. Many

French Catholics fleeing the chaos of that island found a haven in Charleston.

January 3. The new state constitution went into effect.

February 19. Kershaw County was created.

February 19. Camden was incorporated as a city.

February 19. The Jewish Congregation of Beth Elohim in Charleston was incorporated under article 8, section 1 of the new state constitution which granted the free exercise of religion. That same day, the congregation of St. Mary's was incorporated as the Roman Catholic Church of Charleston.

February 19. The right of primogeniture was abolished as of May 1, 1791.

April 27–May 28. President George Washington entered the state at Little River and proceeded to Georgetown, Charleston, and Savannah before returning to the north by Augusta and Columbia.

1792 In the case *Bowman* v. *Middleton*, a South Carolina court declared a state law unconstitutional.

March 9. A branch of the first U.S. Bank was opened in Charleston.

George Washington was reelected. South Carolina cast eight electoral votes for him, seven for John Adams, and one for Aaron Burr.

December 8. Henry Laurens died and was cremated at Mepkin plantation on the Cooper River.

1793   The first year sizable cotton shipments were made from Charleston. The recent invention of the roller gin by Abraham Eve for sea island cotton and the saw-toothed gin by Eli Whitney for upland cotton made the increase in production possible.

April. Citizen Genet arrived in Charleston on his way to Philadelphia to present his credentials as envoy of the new French republic.

1794   Plans for Castle Pinckney which was to be built on Shute's Folly in Charleston harbor were made. Construction began in 1797; work was completed by 1809 when it was considered the strongest fortification in the harbor.

January 13. William Loughton Smith, Charleston district's representative in the U.S. House of Representatives, delivered a great speech on Anglo-American commercial relations. Alexander Hamilton had supplied the facts.

February. Charleston Mechanic Society, founded with 74 members, became the state's first labor organization. The members of the society contributed their labor for the erection of Fort Mechanic on High Battery.

May 10. The Medical Society of South Carolina was incorporated.

1795   *February 26.* Commandant Francis Marion died at Fort Johnson.

July. John Rutledge delivered a fiery speech against the Jay Treaty in St. Michael's Church.

September 13. The Reverend Robert Smith was consecrated the first Episcopal Bishop of South Carolina at Christ Church in Philadelphia.

December 15. The Senate rejected the nomination of John Rutledge to be chief justice of the United States.

1796 *June 13.* Another great Charleston fire devastated the city and consumed many of the houses and public buildings between Bay and Church streets, north from Broad Street to St. Philip's Church.

John Adams elected president. South Carolina had cast eight electoral votes for Thomas Jefferson and eight for Thomas Pinckney. Jefferson squeezed out Pinckney for the vice presidency of the United States.

1797 *October 27.* When one of the French negotiators asked for a "douceur," Charles Cotesworth Pinckney replied: "No, no, not a sixpence." Robert Goodloe Harper coined the phrase "Millions for Defense But Not One Cent for Tribute" as a toast at a banquet in Philadelphia given in John Marshall's honor, June 18, 1798, upon his return to America.

December 16. The Mutual Insurance Company and the Charleston Insurance Company, one for fire and the other for marine insurance, were the first insurance companies incorporated by the state.

1798 *May 5.* A mass meeting was held in St. Michael's Church to consider the threat of an invasion from the French West Indies.

July 19. Governor Charles Pinckney (d. 1824) called the legislators to meet at his home on Meeting Street in Charleston to put the state in a posture of defense.

December 21. Barnwell, Sumter, and Colleton counties were created.

1799 The sloop of war *John Adams* was built in Charleston by public subscription.

February 8. A great celebration in Charleston for the return of Charles Cotesworth Pinckney from France after the "XYZ Affair" culminated in a banquet at City Hall in the Exchange.

December 18. Commissioners were appointed to lay out streets on Sullivan's Island, which had become a summer resort during the 1790s.

December 21. Charleston's first public utility, the Charleston Water Company, was chartered to bring Goose Creek water to Charleston.

1800 **U.S. Census**

White	196,255
Slave	146,151
Free Black	3,185
Total	345,591

January 1. The entire system of courts within the state was reorganized.

January 23. Edward Rutledge was the first governor to die in office. He was succeeded by Lieutenant Governor John Drayton.

July 18. John Rutledge died.

Thomas Jefferson was elected president. South Carolina cast eight electoral votes for him and eight for Aaron Burr.

December 20. A law was passed which made it more difficult to emancipate slaves. Until 1800 a slave could be manumitted by will or deed. After 1800 freeholders of the neighborhood had to certify that the freed person could support his or her family.

1801 Horry County was created out of Georgetown County.

March 17. The Hibernian Society was organized.

December 19. Two state banks were chartered, the Bank of South Carolina and the State Bank.

December 19. The state appropriated $50,000 to pay Phineas Miller and Eli Whitney for the right of South Carolina planters to use their machine called "a saw gin, for cleaning the staple of cotton from the seed." After some difficulties the inventors collected.

December 19. In order to promote greater unity, the legislature chartered a college to be placed at the center of the state. After the Civil War it became the University of South Carolina.

1802 Dr. David Ramsay introduced the practice of vaccination for smallpox to South Carolina.

1803 The corner stone of Fort Dearborn, the Federal Arsenal, was laid near Rocky Mount.

January 10. The *Charleston Courier* began publication. This paper is still published as the *Post and Courier.*

December 17. The foreign slave trade was reopened. More than 40,000 slaves would be imported during the next five years.

December 17. Beaufort was incorporated.

1804 Moses Waddel opened his academy at Willington.

March 26. William Johnson was commissioned an associate justice of the U.S. Supreme Court.

Thomas Jefferson defeated the Federalist Charles Cotesworth Pinckney for the presidency of the United States. South Carolina cast ten electoral votes for Jefferson.

December 6. John Gaillard was elected to the U.S. Senate, where he served until his death on February 26, 1826. He was elected president *pro tempore* on February 28, 1810, and on several later occasions.

1805 *January 10.* The College of South Carolina opened its doors in Columbia.

August 28. Christopher Gadsden, the former leader of the Sons of Liberty, died a Federalist.

September 27. General William Moultrie died.

December 19. Georgetown and Columbia were incorporated.

1806 *October 28.* A Charleston city ordinance restricted the movement of free blacks.

1807 *December.* The embargo went into effect. The commercial life of Charleston never fully recovered from this cessation of foreign trade until after World War II.

1808 Many South Carolina Quakers moved to the Old Northwest in order to escape the institution of slavery.

January 1. The foreign slave trade was brought to an end by federal law, at the earliest possible date under the U.S. Constitution.

October 24. The cornerstone of the Charleston Homespun Company was laid at the west end of Wentworth Street. This, the first manufacturing company in the state, was incorporated on December 15.

James Madison defeated the Federalist Charles Cotesworth Pinckney for the presidency of the United States. South Carolina cast ten electoral votes for Madison.

December 17. An amendment to the state constitution, the result of the "Compromise of 1808," provided for more equal representation between the upcountry and the lowcountry.

1809 *December.* David Ramsay published the two-volume *The History of South-Carolina from its first Settlement in 1670, to the Year 1808.*

1810 The third census of the United States showed that the institution of slavery had spread throughout the state.

White	214,196
Slave	196,365
Free Black	4,554
Total	415,115

December 19. By an amendment to the state constitution "every white man of the age of twenty-one years" could henceforth vote after a residence of six months.

1811 *January 8.* John C. Calhoun married Floride Bonneau Colhoun. This marriage symbolized the growing union of the upcountry and the lowcountry.

December. The South Carolina War Hawks, John C. Calhoun, William Lowndes, and David R. Williams, took their seats in Congress for the first time.

December 12. John C. Calhoun in his maiden speech bombastically called for resentment of every British insult, big or small.

December 21. Free schools were to be established throughout the state.

1812 James Madison was reelected president. South Carolina cast eleven electoral votes for him.

December 19. The Bank of the State of South Carolina was chartered. Although there had been earlier state-chartered banks, this was the first state-owned bank.

December 31. Theodosia Burr Alston, the wife of Governor Joseph Alston, sailed from Georgetown for New York and was never seen again.

1813   *August 22.* The British landed forces at Beaufort and on Hilton Head where marauders plundered settlements.

August 27–28. A great hurricane, surpassed only by those of 1752, 1893, and 1989, struck the South Carolina coast.

1814   *January 19.* Langdon Cheves was elected speaker of the U.S. House of Representatives in succession to Henry Clay.

December 21. The legislature decided to make it easier to change one's name. This could henceforth be done by simply petitioning the courts of the state. The most famous use of this law occurred in 1837 when the Smith brothers of Beaufort changed their name to Rhett.

1815   The Pendleton Farmers' Society was organized. It advocated crop diversification and urged South Carolinians to remain in the state in the face of numerous migrations to the west.

May 6. The historian and physician David Ramsay was shot in the streets of Charleston by William Linner, whom he had ordered to be committed to an institution. Ramsay died on May 8.

1816   Philip Weaver, a master textile mechanic from Coventry, Rhode Island, began the South Carolina Cotton Manufactory in Spartanburg. By 1826 he had left the state because of financial difficulties and his opposition to slavery.

March 22. A treaty with the Cherokees, signed in Washington, D.C., secured the westernmost tip of South Carolina from the Indians. The state approved on December 19, 1816, and by an amendment of the state constitution of December 20, 1820, this land was made a part of Pendleton District.

June. An abortive slave insurrection was thwarted in Camden.

James Monroe was elected president. South Carolina cast eleven electoral votes for him.

December 4. William Smith, the originator of the South Carolina states rights position, was elected to the U.S. Senate where he held a seat until March 3, 1823.

1817   *August 11.* Andrew Pickens died.

December 8. John C. Calhoun took the oath of office as secretary of war.

December 17. Moultrieville on Sullivan's Island was incorporated.

December 17. The state appointed an engineer to superintend public buildings and civil and military works. Thus the state's largest internal improvement program got under way. In 1820 a Board of Public Works was set up which gave way in 1822 to a Superintendent of Public Works. This program of building roads, canals, and courthouses came to a close in 1828 as the railroad emerged on the scene.

1818   *January.* The price of short-staple cotton in the Charleston market reached thirty-five cents per pound, the peak of cotton prices in the antebellum period.

March 28. Wade Hampton III was born in Charleston. His grandfather had put together one of the largest fortunes in America from cotton profits.

1819 *January 6.* The New England Society of Charleston was organized at the Carolina Coffee House at the corner of Tradd Street and Bedon's Alley. New Englanders had been coming to South Carolina to buy cotton for their new mills.

March 6. Langdon Cheves was elected president of the Second Bank of the United States.

May 22. The steamship *Savannah* under the command of Captain Moses Rogers departed Savannah for Liverpool. This was an attempt to reestablish direct trade with England from the southeastern ports.

December 3. Thomas Cooper was elected professor of Chemistry at South Carolina College. A year later he became temporary president and in December 1821 was elected president of the College.

1820 **U.S. Census**

White	237,440
Slave	258,475
Free Black	6,826
Total	502,741

February 14. Charles Pinckney (d. 1824), a representative in Congress, stated that it was not the intention of those who met in Philadelphia in 1787 to have included blacks within the meaning of the word "citizen" in the privileges and immunities clause of the U.S. Constitution.

September 21. John England was consecrated the first Roman Catholic Bishop of South Carolina in St. Finbar's Cathedral in Cork, Ireland. Bishop England landed in Charleston on December 30, 1820. He died April 11, 1842.

James Monroe was reelected president. South Carolina cast eleven electoral votes for him.

December 20. Henceforth no slave could be freed without the formal consent of the state legislature. Nor could free persons of color enter the state.

1821 *May 15.* Sarah Grimké, the eldest daughter of John F. Grimké, sailed for Philadelphia thus making a statement in opposition to slavery.

December 20. A tobacco inspection warehouse was to be built in Hamburg, a new town which had been laid out on the Savannah River by Henry Schultz.

December 20. The South Carolina Academy of Fine Arts was incorporated. A little Greek temple was built on Broad Street in Charleston to house its collection.

December 20. An act authorized the building of a lunatic asylum and a school for the deaf and dumb at or near Columbia. Designed by Robert Mills and embodying new ideas about the treatment of the mentally ill, the asylum received its first patient on December 12, 1828.

1822 Major Alexander Garden (d. 1829) published his *Anecdotes of the Revolutionary War in America.* Thus began the enshrinement of the Revolutionary heroes.

June–July. Fear of a slave insurrection swept Charleston.

June 17, 18. The first arrests were made as the slave insurrection was detected.

June 22. Denmark Vesey, a free black, was apprehended as the ringleader.

June 28. Denmark Vesey was convicted of inciting an insurrection by a court of magistrates and freeholders.

July 2. Denmark Vesey was hanged.

Emanuel African Methodist Episcopal Church Charleston was closed in response to the Vesey insurrection. Reorganized in 1865, it became a focal point for black political activity.

September 27–28. A tremendous hurricane struck the coast near Georgetown. It was worse than the Winyah hurricane of September 10–11, 1820. Many persons on North Island and in the Santee delta were washed away.

November 29. Robert Y. Hayne defeated William Smith for the U.S. Senate.

December 21. A municipal guard of 150 men was formed for Charleston. The Arsenal and Guard House was established in the tobacco inspection warehouse as it was no longer needed since tobacco had declined as a backcountry staple.

December 21. The first of the Seamen Acts was passed. Any free black coming into Charleston on a vessel would be lodged in the local jail during the stay of the vessel in port. If the captain would not pay the cost of board and lodging, the black person could be sold into slavery.

The South Carolina Academy of Fine Arts opened its first exhibition in Charleston.

1823   Construction began on Robert Mills' Fireproof Building in Charleston.

August 7. Judge William Johnson in a federal court decision in the case of *Elkison* v. *Deliesseline* stated that the recent Seamen Act was in conflict with the commerce and treaty-making powers of the U.S. Constitution.

December 20. South Carolina passed a second Seamen Act.

December 20. Two copies of the Great Seal were made, one for the secretary of state's office in Charleston, the other for the secretary of state's office in Columbia, symbolic of the two centers of authority in the state.

1824   The Medical College of South Carolina was founded, but closed in 1838.

Robert Mills was designing courthouses in the "Greek Revival" style, many of which are still standing.

January. The Columbia Canal was completed.

October 29. Charles Pinckney died.

John Quincy Adams was elected president. South Carolina cast eleven electoral votes for Andrew Jackson.

November 21. Modern Reform Judaism was born when members of the Beth Elohim congregation in Charleston organized the Reformed Society of Israelites.

December 17. The legislature created the state's first Court of Appeals. The new three-judge court sat alternately in Columbia and Charleston.

1825 *March.* The Marquis de Lafayette made a triumphal tour through the state. He reached Fayetteville, North Carolina, on March 4, then proceeded to Cheraw, Camden, Columbia, and Charleston whence he sailed to Savannah on March 17.

March. Joel R. Poinsett appointed minister to Mexico. A showy Mexican plant was named poinsettia.

March 4. John C. Calhoun was sworn in as vice president of the United States.

May 23. Parson Weems, the greatest of the mythmakers, died in Beaufort.

August 16. Charles Cotesworth Pinckney died.

December 15–16. The house and senate of South Carolina adopted resolutions protesting against a broad interpretation of the taxing and spending powers of the federal government.

1826 Daniel Blake and Charles Baring established summer homes at Flat Rock, North Carolina, which now could be reached by a road constructed as part of the internal improvements scheme.

Pickens County and Anderson County were created out of Pendleton district.

December 20. The first South Carolina Bar Association was incorporated.

1827 Robert Turnbull published "The Crisis" essays.

February–March. Robert Y. Hayne spoke out in the U.S. Senate against federal appropriations for the American Colonization Society.

July 2. Thomas Cooper, president of South Carolina College, delivered a speech in Columbia in which he questioned the political relationship between the North and South.

November. Edgar Allan Poe began a year's garrison duty at Fort Moultrie on Sullivan's Island. During this period he gathered material for his story "The Gold Bug."

December 19. The South Carolina Canal and Rail Road Company was chartered.

1828 *February.* The *Southern Review* began publication in Charleston. It continued until 1832.

November 2. Thomas Pinckney died.

Andrew Jackson was elected president and John C. Calhoun was elected vice president. South Carolina cast eleven electoral votes for them.

December 19. The legislature adopted the Exposition and Protest (secretly written by Vice President Calhoun) which argued the unconstitutionality of the protective tariff.

1829 The lower portion of "The State Road" that eventually linked Columbia and Charleston was completed.

Daniel A. Payne, a free black, opened a school for black children in Charleston (see 1835 and 1865).

Fort Sumter was begun in Charleston harbor.

The Reverend William Capers began his Methodist mission to the slaves.

July 23. An abortive slave insurrection was discovered and thwarted in Georgetown County.

November. Angelina Grimké, the youngest of Judge Grimké's daughters, left her native state to join her sister Sarah in the North where the Grimké sisters became foremost among the abolitionists.

1830 **U.S. Census**

White	257,863
Black	323,322
Total	581,185

January 19–27. Senator Robert Y. Hayne answered Senator Daniel Webster in a great forensic duel.

April 13. At a Thomas Jefferson birthday celebration in Washington, D.C., President Andrew Jackson toasted: "Our Federal Union—It must be preserved." Vice President John C. Calhoun replied: "The Union—Next to our liberties the most dear."

July 22. The South Carolina Academy of Fine Arts closed.

1831 *July 26.* John C. Calhoun wrote a letter to the *Pendleton Messenger* openly avowing his nullification philosophy.

September. The price of short staple cotton in the Charleston market reached the bottom price of nine cents per pound.

October. John James Audubon and John Bachman met in Charleston. Their friendship nurtured a closer study of nature. Two Audubon sons married Bachman daughters.

December 17. The Medical College of the State of South Carolina was chartered. It opened in 1833.

1832 Caroline Gilman began editing *The Rose Bud, or Youth's Gazette,* the first children's paper in the country.

June 1. The last of the Revolutionary war heroes, Thomas Sumter, died.

July 14. Congress passed the Tariff of 1832 which helped to set the nullification crisis in motion.

August 28. Calhoun explained further his nullification doctrine in a letter to Governor James Hamilton.

September 21. Sir Walter Scott, who with Parson Weems had been such a great influence on the mind of the South, died.

October 30. The brig *Amelia,* sailing from New York to New Orleans, grounded off Folly Island. An outbreak of cholera killed about twenty of the passengers and posed a threat of epidemic to Charleston. The crew and passengers were quarantined and the vessel was burnt.

Andrew Jackson was reelected president. South

Carolina cast eleven electoral votes for John Floyd.

November 19–24. The Nullification Convention met in Columbia.

November 24. The Ordinance of Nullification nullified the tariff acts of 1828 and 1832. "An Address to the People of South Carolina" by Robert J. Turnbull and "An Address to the States of the Union" by John C. Calhoun and George McDuffie were also adopted.

December 10. Jackson issued his proclamation condemning treason in South Carolina.

December 21. Governor Hayne, who had just succeeded Hamilton, issued his own counter-proclamation.

December 28. Calhoun resigned as vice president of the United States to resume his seat in the U.S. Senate.

1833 *January 4.* Calhoun took his seat in the U.S. Senate.

January 21. A convention assembled in Charleston to postpone the date on which the Ordinance of Nullification was to have gone into effect (February 1, 1833).

March 2. Congress passed and the president signed the Tariff of 1833 and the Force Bill into law.

March 15. The Ordinance of Nullification was repealed and on March 18 the Force Act nullified.

October. The steam railroad from Charleston to Hamburg was completed, a distance of 136 miles (at that time it was the longest railroad in the world).

December 19. Capital punishment for "a slave or a free person of color" was restricted to hanging.

1834 *June 2.* Unionist judges John Belton O'Neall and David Johnson on the South Carolina Court of Appeals declared the militia oath void, because it violated the U.S. Constitution. William Harper dissented.

October. Thomas Smith Grimké died in Ohio.

December 9. Thomas Cooper resigned the presidency of South Carolina College.

December 17. The Saluda Manufacturing Company was incorporated. Employing slave labor, it became the largest cotton factory in the state. It was burned by Sherman.

1835 *February 14.* St. Philip's Church in Charleston was destroyed by fire. The present church was built in 1838.

April. In New York, William Gilmore Simms's *The Yemassee* was published and became a great success.

May. Daniel A. Payne closed his school for blacks in Charleston and left the state.

July. The Bank of Charleston was founded. It became the largest in the state at that time.

July 29–30. A mob raided the Charleston post office in order to prevent the circulation of abolitionist pamphlets through the mails.

Francis Lieber, the political philosopher, arrived in Columbia before October to begin twenty-one years of teaching at South Carolina College.

1836   Thomas Cooper and David J. McCord began to publish *The Statutes at Large of South Carolina* in ten volumes. Publication was completed in 1841.

February 4. Henry Laurens Pinckney presented resolutions in the U.S. House of Representatives which would become the "gag rule."

May 18. A select committee reported on Pinckney's resolutions and the "gag rule" was adopted by a 117–68 vote.

September–November. A major cholera epidemic ravaged Charleston.

Martin Van Buren was elected president. South Carolina cast eleven electoral votes for Willie P. Mangum of North Carolina.

1837   William Harper published his *Memoir on Slavery* as an antidote to abolitionist writings.

January 3. The state's most versatile post-Civil War business man, James Lide Coker, was born.

February 6. Calhoun defended slavery in the U.S. Senate as "a positive good."

March 6. The Senate confirmed the appointment of Joel R. Poinsett as secretary of war by President Van Buren.

1838 John Lyde Wilson published *The Code of Honor* for conducting duels.

January 30. Osceola, the Seminole Indian chief, died in captivity at Fort Moultrie.

April 27–28. Another great fire in Charleston destroyed Ansonborough. The houses built after this fire have undergone notable restoration beginning in the 1960s.

November 27. Angelica Singleton, daughter of Richard Singleton of Richland County, married Abram Van Buren, eldest son of President Martin Van Buren. The president being a widower, Angelica Singleton Van Buren often acted as First Lady.

1839 Erskine College was founded but did not obtain a state charter until 1850.

Theodore Weld published *American Slavery As It Is* with a number of stories drawn from the knowledge of the Grimké sisters.

The College of Charleston became the first municipally funded college in the United States.

1840 **U.S. Census**

White	259,084
Slave	327,038
Free Black	8,276
Total	594,398

Reputedly designed by Robert Mills, the first American college library under a separate roof was completed at South Carolina College (now the Caroliniana Library).

March 13. The Nation Ford Treaty between the Catawba Indians and the state concluded in York District would become the basis for the Catawba land suit in 1980.

William H. Harrison was elected president. South Carolina cast eleven electoral votes for Martin Van Buren.

1841 Dr. N. P. Walker opened a school for the deaf at Cedar Springs near Spartanburg. The facility was expanded in 1855 to include education for the blind. In 1856 it became a state institution.

1842 *March.* Ex-President Martin Van Buren visited South Carolina and the family of his daughter-in-law Angelica Singleton at their plantation near Stateburg in Sumter County.

June 28. Railroad service between Charleston and Columbia began with the arrival in Columbia of the *Robert Y. Hayne.*

December 20. The Citadel, a military college, was established in Charleston.

1844 The Methodists split into northern and southern churches over the question of whether a bishop might own slaves or not.

April 1. Calhoun entered upon his duties as secretary of state in President John Tyler's Cabinet.

July 31. At a dinner in Bluffton in St. Luke's parish, Robert Barnwell Rhett launched the Bluffton movement for a state convention and separate state action on the tariff.

James K. Polk was elected president. South Carolina cast nine electoral votes for him.

November 28. Judge Samuel Hoar of Massachusetts came to protest the Seamen Acts, but was driven out of the state.

1845 The Baptists in the nation split over the question of slavery.

November. Calhoun was made president of the Memphis commercial convention.

December 15. Under William Gregg's direction, the Graniteville Manufacturing Company was chartered.

1846 *May 13.* War was declared on Mexico. South Carolina's Palmetto Regiment served with distinction.

August 8. David Wilmot of Pennsylvania urged a proviso to a wartime appropriations act stating that neither slavery nor involuntary servitude should exist in any territory acquired from Mexico.

1847 *January 15.* Rhett in the U.S. House of Representatives opposed the Wilmot Proviso.

February 19. Calhoun in the U.S. Senate opposed the Wilmot Proviso.

March 9. The Palmetto Regiment landed at Tampico, Mexico. It suffered heavy casualties in several battles; only about half the men survived the war.

May 10. A public dinner for Daniel Webster was held in St. Andrews Hall, Charleston.

August 11. Benjamin R. Tillman was born.

August 20. Former governor Pierce M. Butler was killed while leading the Palmetto Regiment at the battle of Churubusco.

September 13. The Palmetto flag was the first U.S. flag to be planted on the walls of Mexico City.

1848 Judge John Belton O'Neall completed codification of *The Negro Law of South Carolina.*

July. The telegraph connection was completed between Columbia and Charleston.

July 27. A celebration was held in Columbia in honor of the Palmetto Regiment, which was returning from the Mexican War.

November. Zachary Taylor was elected president. South Carolina cast nine electoral votes for Lewis Cass.

1849 The German Colonization Society of Charleston, under the direction of John A. Wagener, purchased land for a German settlement at Walhalla.

July 13–14. After a massive jailbreak by slaves in Charleston, a mob threatened to burn the Episcopal Calvary Church under construction to serve the black community.

1850 **U.S. Census**

White	274,563
Black	393,944
Total	668,507

March 4. Calhoun made his last speech in the U.S. Senate with the hope of saving the Union.

March 31. Calhoun died in Washington, D.C.

April 25–26. Calhoun was buried in the western cemetery of St. Philip's Church after lying in state at City Hall.

June 3–12. Southern extremists met in convention at Nashville to condemn the Compromise of 1850 and promote Southern secession. Robert Barnwell Rhett was the outspoken leader of the South Carolina delegation. When the second session met November 11–18, Langdon Cheves, a more moderate South Carolinian, spoke in favor of secession only if all southern states went out together.

December 20. Furman University, a Baptist institution, was chartered. It opened in Greenville in 1852.

1851 Wofford College, a Methodist institution named for Benjamin Wofford, its first large benefactor, was chartered in 1851 and opened in Spartanburg in 1854.

February 10–11. An election was held for delegates to a state convention scheduled for April 1852 to consider separate state action.

May 5–8. The Southern Rights Association in favor of secession met in Charleston.

July 29. The Cooperationists, who would only secede if the South went as one, met in Charleston.

September 23. A second meeting of the Cooperationists was held in Charleston.

October 13, 14. In this statewide election the people voted against separate state action. The state stepped back from the abyss of secession.

December 15. The cornerstone for the third State House was laid. This building, though substantially completed before the war, was not completely finished until 1907.

1852 *April 26.* The state convention which had been elected in February 1851 to consider separate state action met in Columbia.

April 30. In a letter to Governor John H. Means, Robert B. Rhett resigned his seat in the U.S. Senate.

July. Columbia and Greenville were joined by rail.

September. Columbia's original Sidney Park was named for Algernon Sidney Johnston.

November. South Carolina cast nine electoral votes for Franklin Pierce, who became president.

1854 William Grayson's "The Hireling and the Slave" was published.

Greenville Baptist Female College was established. In 1938 it merged with Furman University.

December. James L. Petigru won a case for an alleged Yankee abolitionist who had been abused by vigilantes in St. Bartholomew parish.

1855 *June 2.* The South Carolina Historical Society was established.

August 3. John R. Niernsee was selected as architect of the State House.

December 19. Clarendon County was created.

1856 Charleston established a public school system which was modeled after New York schools by C. G. Memminger and W. J. Bennett.

March 17. The Mt. Vernon Ladies Association organized by Ann Pamela Cunningham of Laurens County was chartered. She began the project in 1853 and the association purchased George Washington's home in 1858.

May 19. Massachusetts Senator Charles Sumner delivered his "The Crime against Kansas" speech in which he castigated South Carolina Senator Andrew Butler.

May 22. Congressman Preston Brooks, a nephew of Senator Butler, hit Charles Sumner thirty times over the head with a gutta percha walking cane while the Senator from Massachusetts was sitting at his desk in the U.S. Senate.

November. The first State Fair was held in Columbia.

November. James Buchanan was elected president. South Carolina cast eight electoral votes for him.

December 20. Newberry College, a Lutheran institution, was chartered. It opened to students in 1859.

1857 *December 7.* James L. Orr was elected Speaker of the U.S. House of Representatives.

1858 *March 4.* Senator James H. Hammond proclaimed "Cotton is King" during debates in the U.S. Senate.

1859 Columbia Female College (now called Columbia College), a Methodist institution, received its first students.

John Belton O'Neall published *Bench and Bar* in two volumes.

V. SECESSION, WAR, AND AFTER (1860–1895)

In December 1860 South Carolina had voted unanimously to secede from the Union. The state then sent commissioners to the other Southern states to urge them to secede and join in the formation of the Confederate States of America. Six followed South Carolina. The victory at Fort Sumter on April 14, 1861, brought four more Southern states into the Confederacy. Carolinians who had rushed into secession supported first Francis W. Pickens and then Milledge L. Bonham, both of whom were from Edgefield, as governors of the state. But in December 1864 the reluctant secessionists swept back into power under the leadership of Andrew Gordon Magrath of Charleston.

Except for the sea islands around Beaufort, the state was spared federal occupation until General Sherman commenced his march of destruction from Savannah to Columbia. Both Charleston and Columbia were taken by federal troops on February 17, 1865.

The Civil War was a catastrophe for South Carolina. Not only were many of the best and bravest men of the state killed or maimed, but the economic and social system of nearly two centuries was wrecked forever. When the war was over the federal government, with extraordinary ineptitude, tried to establish state government by white administrators from the North, by a few white South Carolinians who had remained loyal to the Union and by blacks. Although this "Reconstruction" government was well-intentioned and achieved some good things, little attempt was made to involve the acknowledged leaders of the white community who were experienced and responsible and no effort was made to create an alternative economic base for the state. Although some blacks showed considerable ability, most of them had no training in administration and no satisfactory source of livelihood once they were freed from their white masters. South Carolinians had grown accustomed to conservative government which, if it was hierarchic and sometimes obtuse, was also remarkably honest and thrifty. Between 1868 and 1876 the Reconstruction legislature did pass laws relative to financial reform, the building of penal and charitable institutions, and the establishment of the public school system.

When federal troops were withdrawn in 1877 South Carolinians were again allowed to govern themselves. Political power alternated uncertainly between representatives of the old gentry class on one hand, such as Wade Hampton, Duncan Clinch Heyward, and Richard I. Manning, who, moderate and reasonable as they were, could do little to revive the crippled economy, and flamboyant demagogues on the other hand, such as Ben Tillman and "Coley" Blease, who did incalculable harm by playing on the fears and resentments of the impoverished and demoralized whites. During the 1880s textile mills, which had been present in the western part of the state since before the Civil War, grew into a major industry. The plight of many blacks appeared worse at this time than it had been under slavery, for they now lived in a society that simply had no jobs for them. Many whites wished that the blacks would simply go away and they embodied their feelings in segregation laws and customs. Acceptance of the black citizens' rights and place in the society was retarded by laws that resulted in their disenfranchisement and segregation. The march toward this segregation of society culminated in the Constitution of 1895 which effectively permitted the blacks to be ruled out of the political life of the state.

1860 U.S. Census

Whites	291,300
Slaves	402,406
Free Blacks	9,914
Others	88
Total	703,708

April 16–17. The state Democratic convention met in Columbia to select delegates to attend the national Democratic convention which would be held in Charleston.

April 23. The national Democratic convention met in Charleston. On April 28 eight Southern delegations walked out in a dispute over the platform. South Carolina delegates remained.

November 1860–August 1865. Mary Boykin Chesnut of Camden kept a diary of her wartime life with commentary upon the times. The Chesnut Diary has become a Civil War classic.

Abraham Lincoln was elected president. South Carolina cast eight electoral votes for John C. Breckinridge.

November 6. News of Lincoln's election reached Charleston.

November 7. Federal District Judge Andrew Magrath and Federal District Attorney James Conner resigned their offices.

December 6. The delegates were elected to the Secession Convention.

December 17. The Secession Convention opened in Columbia at the First Baptist Church but removed to Charleston because of a smallpox epidemic in Columbia.

December 20. The state of South Carolina "in convention assembled" at St. Andrews Hall in Charleston voted unanimously (169–0) to secede from the Union. The members signed the Ordinance of Secession the same evening in Institute Hall.

December 26. Major Robert Anderson moved the federal troops in Charleston Harbor from Fort Moultrie to Fort Sumter.

1861 *January 4.* South Carolina sent commissioners to each Southern state.

January 8. South Carolina's first casualty was suffered at Castle Pinckney where a soldier was accidentally shot.

January 9. The Citadel Cadets stationed on Morris Island fired upon the U.S. vessel *Star of the West,* which was bringing supplies to Fort Sumter.

February 9. South Carolina joined other Southern states in Montgomery, Alabama, to form the Confederate States of America.

March 3. General Pierre G. T. Beauregard arrived in Charleston to take command of the Confederate troops.

April 12. The first shot was fired on Fort Sumter.

April 14. Major Robert Anderson surrendered Fort Sumter to General Beauregard.

April 19. President Lincoln proclaimed a blockade of the Confederate ports.

May 11. With the arrival of the USS *Niagara,* the U.S. naval blockade of Charleston began.

October 12. Confederate commissioners James Mason and John Slidell left Charleston for Europe aboard the blockade runner *Theodora.*

November 7. The Union fleet sailed past Hilton Head Island into Port Royal Sound. The planters abandoned the Sea Islands. The slaves therefore became de facto freemen.

December 11. A great fire swept through Charleston from the Cooper River at East Bay north of the market to the corner of Tradd and Rutledge on the Ashley River.

December 19–20. Union forces sank sixteen stone and granite loaded ships in Charleston harbor to obstruct passage. This "stone fleet" was augmented by an additional thirteen vessels sunk January 25–26, 1862.

1862 Penn Normal and Industrial School, founded at Frogmore on St. Helena Island by northern missionaries, began the education of the blacks on the Sea Islands. This school was incorporated into the Beaufort County system in the 1940s.

May 13. Robert Smalls, a black pilot, with a black crew sailed in the Confederate steamer *Planter* out of Charleston and joined the Union fleet.

June 16. The Confederates at Secessionville on James Island repulsed a Union attack.

November. The first black regiment was mustered into service in South Carolina. The First Regiment of South Carolina Volunteers was commanded by Colonel Thomas W. Higginson, a white man from Massachusetts. During the war over 5,000 black South Carolinians joined the Union Army.

December. Milledge L. Bonham was elected governor.

1863 *January 1.* Emancipation Day, which has since been celebrated annually by South Carolina blacks.

January 30. The Union gunboat *Isaac Smith* was forced aground by Confederate batteries on the Stono River near Legareville and captured.

March 9. James L. Petigru, South Carolina's leading Unionist, died. He was buried with full honors from the city of Charleston and the Confederate military.

April 7. Admiral Samuel Francis Du Pont attacked Fort Sumter.

June 2. Harriet Tubman led Union troops in a raid up the Combahee River. This is the only time a woman has led American troops in battle.

July 10. Union forces began an assault on Fort Wagner on Morris Island. Confederate forces evacuated the island September 6.

July 18. In the charge of the 54th Massachusetts against Fort Wagner, Robert Gould Shaw was killed as well as many former slaves who were now fighting for their freedom.

August 22. The Swamp Angel, a gun on Morris Island, began to lob shells into the city of Charleston as far north as Calhoun Street.

September 8–9. A boat attack was launched against Fort Sumter.

October 5. The submarine *David* attacked the USS *New Ironsides.*

October 26–December 6. The second great bombardment of Fort Sumter ensued unremitted for forty-one days and nights.

November 2. Jefferson Davis, president of the Confederacy, visited Charleston.

November 28. The Mills House in Charleston closed because of the danger posed by Union shelling.

1864 *February 17.* The submarine *Hunley* sank the USS *Housatonic* but was also lost.

May 12. Wade Hampton was named commander of the Confederate Cavalry Corps upon the death of J. E. B. Stuart. He was not formally appointed until August 11.

July 7. The third and final great bombardment of Fort Sumter began.

December. Andrew Gordon Magrath was elected the last governor under the state's 1790 constitution.

December 24. General William T. Sherman took Savannah.

1865   St. Mark's Episcopal Church organized by a black congregation was established in Charleston.

Daniel A. Payne returned to Charleston as the bishop appointed to establish the African Methodist Episcopal Church in the state.

January–February. Sherman marched through South Carolina from Savannah to Columbia.

January 16. Sherman issued Special Field Order No. 15 appropriating the Sea Islands and coastal lands for freed slaves. General Rufus Saxton was given the task of assigning the head of each family forty acres and the temporary use of a military horse or mule. This probably was the origin of the expression "forty acres and a mule."

February 3–4. The battle of Rivers Bridge near Ehrhardt on the Salkehatchie River slowed the Union army's march to Columbia but cost approximately 200 Confederate and 400 Union casualties.

February 17. Federal troops took Charleston and Columbia the same day.

February 17. During the evacuation of Charleston the Confederate ironclad *Palmetto State* was blown up, a cloud of smoke billowing up in the form of a palmetto.

February 18. There was a great explosion at the Northeastern Railroad depot in Charleston. Columbia burned.

February 24. Union troops occupied Georgetown.

March 1. The *Harvest Moon* was sunk by a mine in Winyah Bay.

March 3. Congress established the Freedmen's Bureau. The life of the Bureau was extended on July 18, 1866, and it functioned in South Carolina until June 30, 1872.

April 5–21. General Edward Potter led a raid into the interior of the state from Georgetown.

April 14. Robert Anderson raised the U.S. flag over Fort Sumter four years to the day after he surrendered. The Reverend Henry Ward Beecher delivered the oration on that occasion.

April 14. President Lincoln was assassinated.

May 2. Jefferson Davis held the last Confederate council of war at the home of Armistead Burt in Abbeville.

June 30. President Andrew Johnson issued a proclamation establishing a provisional government for South Carolina. He named Benjamin F. Perry the provisional governor.

July 18. Major General Quincy A. Gillmore assumed command of the military department of South Carolina.

September 13–27. A convention met in Columbia and drew up the Constitution of 1865. The "Black Codes" were adopted under its authority. Article XI abolished state offices in Charleston, thereby centralizing government in Columbia.

1865 *October 1.* Avery Normal Institute was organized by Francis L. Cardozo.

November 13. South Carolina ratified the Thirteenth Amendment which had freed the slaves.

November 18. General Daniel E. Sickles replaced Gillmore as commander of the Department of South Carolina.

November 29. James L. Orr was inaugurated governor under the Constitution of 1865.

December. Former Governor Magrath was released from Fort Pulaski near Savannah.

1866 Dexter E. Converse became manager of the Converse Manufacturing Company near Spartanburg, a textile mill.

The Confederate Memorial Association was organized.

The crop-lien system was given legal sanction.

January 1. General Sickles declared the "Black Codes" void.

December 19. South Carolina rejected the Fourteenth Amendment—the Senate unanimously and the House with but one vote for it.

December 20. Legislation was passed to establish an immigration commissioner to encourage immigration of European whites to try to offset the black majority.

1867 Phosphates were discovered in the lowcountry and thus arose one of the state's first postwar industries.

The Central Correctional Institution was constructed at Columbia on the banks of the Congaree River.

March 2. The Second Military District was established consisting of South Carolina and North Carolina with Major General Daniel E. Sickles in command.

August 31. Major General E. R. S. Canby succeeded General Sickles in command of the Second District.

November 19–20. The first election in which the freedmen fully participated was held to elect state and local officials. The election lists provided the first records of the full names of freedmen.

1868   The Governor's Mansion, formerly the officers' quarters of the Arsenal Academy, became the official residence of the state's chief executive. Robert K. Scott was the first occupant.

January 14–March 18. A convention drew up the Constitution of 1868. The convention was composed of seventy-six blacks and forty-eight whites.

January 29. Oconee County was created.

April 16. Justus K. Jillson of Massachusetts was elected the first superintendent of education, an office created by the Constitution of 1868.

June 2–3. The first general election was held under the Constitution of 1868.

July 6. Governor James L. Orr retired from the governorship to make way for Robert K. Scott of Ohio.

July 9. Francis L. Cardozo became the state's first black secretary of state.

July 9. South Carolina ratified the Fourteenth Amendment.

July 24. Military rule ended as General Canby resigned his authority to the new civil government.

August 19. Circuit courts were created throughout the state.

November. Ulysses S. Grant was elected president. South Carolina cast six electoral votes for him.

1869 The Highland Park Hotel was built at Aiken and became an important destination for wealthy northern tourists.

The *Rural Carolinian* began publication under the editorship of D. Wyatt Aiken.

December 18. Claflin, the state's oldest African-American college, was founded at Orangeburg.

1870 U.S. Census

Whites	289,667
Blacks	415,814
Others	125
Total	705,606

February 1. Jonathan Jasper Wright became the first black elected to the South Carolina Supreme

Court. He served until his resignation December 1, 1877.

June 11. William Gilmore Simms, South Carolina's most influential antebellum writer, died.

July 1. James W. Smith of South Carolina became the first black student to enter the U.S. Military Academy at West Point.

November 28. Alonzo J. Ransier became the first black South Carolinian to be elected to the office of lieutenant governor.

December 12. Representative Joseph H. Rainey was the first black South Carolinian to be sworn in as a member of the U.S. Congress.

1871 The Grange was established in South Carolina.

Benedict Institute, a Baptist college, was founded in Columbia.

March 6. A General School Act was passed.

March 10. Aiken County was created from parts of Edgefield, Barnwell, Orangeburg, and Lexington counties.

May 9. The first Taxpayers Convention was held in Columbia.

October 17. President Ulysses S. Grant issued a proclamation suspending the writ of habeas corpus in nine South Carolina counties under authority granted to him in the act of April 20, 1871.

1872 *The Revised Statutes of South Carolina* were completed.

September 21. John Henry Conyers was the first black South Carolinian to enter the U.S. Naval Academy at Annapolis.

November. Ulysses S. Grant was reelected president. South Carolina cast seven electoral votes for him.

1873 *October 7.* Henry E. Hayne was the first black accepted as a student at the University of South Carolina.

1874 The *Greenville Daily News* established by A. M. Speights became the *Greenville News* October 26, 1920.

February 17. The second Taxpayers Convention was held in Columbia.

Daniel H. Chamberlain was elected governor.

1875 *July 10.* Mary McLeod Bethune was born at Mayesville.

1876 *July 8.* At least one white and four blacks were killed in a race riot in the industrial town of Hamburg.

August 18. Pickens County Democrats held the state's first primary election.

September 16–19. At least one white and about forty blacks were killed in race riots at Ellenton in Aiken County.

October 7. Governor Daniel H. Chamberlain disbanded the extralegal white militia.

October 17. President Grant issued a proclamation which placed federal troops at the call of Governor Chamberlain.

November. The tempestuous and disputed gubernatorial election between the incumbent Chamberlain and Wade Hampton took place.

Rutherford B. Hayes was elected president. South Carolina's seven electoral votes were disputed but eventually counted for Hayes.

November 28. Federal troops occupied the State House.

December 7. While Chamberlain was being inaugurated, Wade Hampton delivered a speech in which he said, "The people have elected me Governor, and by the Eternal God, I will be Governor or we shall have a military Governor."

December 14. Wade Hampton, disputing Chamberlain's election, took the oath of office as governor.

Henry Martyn Robert published "Robert's Rules of Order."

1877   *April 10.* President Hayes ordered federal troops withdrawn from Columbia. Chamberlain conceded the gubernatorial dispute, leaving Hampton as governor.

June 7. The Fence Law permitted enclosures, thus preventing cattle from grazing freely. (It did not apply to the entire state until 1921.)

1878   *February 18.* Hampton County was created from part of Beaufort.

March 1. The General Assembly passed legislation to end public executions.

March. The University of South Carolina was divided into two branches: whites attended in Columbia, blacks in Orangeburg.

December 10. Wade Hampton was elected to the U.S. Senate.

December 23. The State Board of Health was established.

December 24. The State Railroad Commission was established.

1880 **U.S. Census**

White	391,105
Black	604,332
Other	140
Total	995,577

The 1880 census was the only federal census in which the state's black population exceeded 60 percent.

The Women's Christian Temperance Union was organized in South Carolina. Sallie F. Chapin was the first president.

July 5. W. M. Shannon was killed in a duel by E. B. C. Cash. Legislation enacted in December 1880 made dueling henceforth a crime.

November. James A. Garfield was elected president. South Carolina cast seven electoral votes for Winfield S. Hancock, the Democratic candidate.

1881 Allen University, a Methodist institution, moved to Columbia.

Charleston investors Francis Pelzer and Ellison Smyth established the Pelzer Manufacturing Company on the Saluda River in Anderson County.

April 9. Martin Witherspoon Gary died.

December 5. Carrie T. Pollitzer, pioneer leader of women's rights movement, was born in Charleston.

December 6. The University of South Carolina Alumni Association was created.

1882 *January 30.* Berkeley County was created from a part of Charleston County.

The Pacolet Manufacturing Company was created by John H. Montgomery and C. E. Fleming. It initiated a much greater involvement of New England and New York engineering, machinery, and commission house business in the South Carolina textile industry.

February 9. The "Eight Box Voting law" was employed to reduce black participation.

July 5. The Dibble Plan created one large low-country district to ensure the election of a black congressman.

1884 *May.* The University of South Carolina Law School reopened with Joseph D. Pope as head.

November. Grover Cleveland was elected president. South Carolina cast nine electoral votes for him.

December 11. The South Carolina Bar Association was incorporated.

1885 *August 6.* Benjamin Ryan Tillman made a stunning speech on the plight of the farmer at Bennettsville before the State Grange and the State Agricultural and Mechanical Society.

1886 *August 31.* Ninety-two persons died in an earthquake that caused enormous property damage in Charleston.

December 23. South Carolina passed a general incorporation law.

1888 *November.* Benjamin Harrison was elected president. South Carolina cast nine electoral votes for Grover Cleveland.

December 22. Florence County was created from parts of Marion, Darlington, Williamsburg, and Clarendon counties.

1889 *May 21.* The Federal Circuit Court of Appeals validated the will of Thomas G. Clemson who had left money for the founding of an institution of higher learning at the former home of John C. Calhoun.

Converse College was founded in Spartanburg. It opened to students October 1, 1890.

December 14. Wofford defeated Furman five goals to one in the state's first intercollegiate football game.

1890 **U.S. Census**

White	462,008
Black	688,934
Other	207
Total	1,151,149

January 23. The "Shell Manifesto," written by Tillman, issued a call for a convention of the Farmers' Movement.

November 3. In the "Revolution of 1890" Tillman populists defeated the aristocratic old guard at the polls.

December 11. The Tillman-controlled state legislature selected John L. M. Irby to replace Wade Hampton in the U.S. Senate.

1891 *February.* The State Society of the Daughters of the American Revolution was formed.

February 18. The first issue of *The State* was issued with N. G. Gonzales as manager and editor.

June. The Marines established a training base on Parris Island.

1892 *November.* Grover Cleveland was elected president. South Carolina cast nine electoral votes for him.

December 24. The legislature limited the hours of work in cotton and woolen factories to sixty-six per week or eleven a day.

December 24. The Dispensary system of selling liquor went into effect. This state monopoly lasted until 1907.

1893 Mount Vernon Mills opened the nation's first totally electrified textile plant at Columbia. In 1981 the building was donated to the state to house the State Museum.

July 6. Clemson College received its first students.

August 27 and *October 13.* Severe hurricanes swept the state; over 1,000 lives were lost in the coastal areas.

December 1. By this date the Tillman Movement had cleared the state's benches of all Hampton justices.

1894 Sara Campbell Allen became the first woman physician in South Carolina.

President Grover Cleveland came to Georgetown to shoot ducks. When a stiff gale overturned his skiff, national attention was focused upon South Carolina as a hunting preserve. Wealthy Yankee sportsmen began to come south for the winter.

March 30. In Darlington there was a riot between constables who were enforcing the new liquor laws and local citizens who resented their doing so.

August 1. Benjamin E. Mays, minister, educator, and civil rights leader, was born in Rambo, South Carolina.

October 8. In the *State ex rel. George* v. *Aiken* decision the Tillmanite-controlled state supreme court declared the Dispensary system constitutional.

November 6. George Washington Murray, South Carolina's last black Congressman until 1992, was elected to the House.

November 7. The state's first chapter of the United Daughters of the Confederacy was organized.

December 27. The State Historical Commission was established.

1895 Construction began on Olympia Mill in Columbia. Upon completion it contained over 100,000 spindles, the world's largest textile mill under one roof.

March 4. Tillman entered the U.S. Senate, where he sat until his death on July 3, 1918.

September 10–December 4. A convention drew up the Constitution of 1895.

September 24. Frances Guignard Gibbes of Columbia became the first woman allowed to take a course at the University of South Carolina. Three years later, Mattie Jean Adams became the first woman to graduate from the University.

October 15. Winthrop Normal College for Women in Rock Hill, created by the state legislature in 1891, received its first students.

October 25. Thomas E. Miller, one of six black delegates, addressed the Constitutional Convention in support of unrestricted suffrage.

December 4. The Constitution of 1895 was adopted by the Convention, but it was not sent to the people for ratification.

VI. THE SEGREGATED STATE
(1896–1964)

Exhausted soils, hurricanes, the boll weevil, and a general depression in the prices of agricultural products kept South Carolina poor when other sections of the nation were prospering. Nevertheless, among blacks and whites of all classes some of the old appreciation of beauty and gaiety remained. Having less money than other Americans, South Carolinians were less likely to appraise an individual by his income and more likely to judge him by the strength of his character.

South Carolina may be said to have truly rejoined the nation in 1930. A severe economic depression which followed the stock market crash in 1929 brought the American standard of living down to the point where the chronic poverty of South Carolina was no longer so remarkable, and the energetic and levelheaded James F. Byrnes was elected to the United States Senate. In 1932 a Democrat with some Southern sympathies, Franklin Delano Roosevelt, was elected president and thus the Democratic Party of South Carolina at last became a branch of a nationwide political party that was in power.

The federal government poured money into the state, many public works were undertaken, pellagra was virtually eliminated, malaria greatly reduced, and hookworm infestation curbed. In World War II, rising prices for farm products and war-related industrialization brought prosperity to the state for the first time since before the Civil War.

After the war blacks were no longer willing to accept the most extreme indignities of segregation. While impetuous whites wasted their energies in futile attempts to resist the achievement of civil rights for blacks, more moderate leaders generally prevented violent confrontations. After the famous 1954 Supreme Court decision which began the end of segregation in the schools, the state needed more than ten years to adjust. Clemson University admitted Harvey Gantt in 1964 as its first black student and by the end of 1965 the University of South Carolina had opened its doors to all of the state's citizens. The Civil Rights Acts of 1964 and 1965 and the Voting Rights Act of 1965 marked the beginning of a new era. The computer revolution also began in the middle of the 1960s, speeding up the rate of change in banking, business, and government affairs. In the 1960s the leadership in the state was extraordinarily successful in attracting new industries to the state, especially foreign-owned industries which introduced a cosmopolitan awareness into the state's social and intellectual life. Air-conditioning improved summer working conditions which eased some of the tensions in the rapidly industrializing state.

1896   *February 25.* Saluda County was created from part of Edgefield.

March 3. The General Assembly established the State College for Negroes at Orangeburg. Thomas E. Miller, a former black congressman, served as its first president.

May 28. The U.S. Supreme Court in *Plessy* v. *Ferguson* upheld segregation.

August 25. South Carolina held the nation's first statewide primary election.

November. William McKinley was elected president. South Carolina cast nine electoral votes for William Jennings Bryan.

November 12. The University of South Carolina defeated Clemson 12–6 in the first "Big Thursday" football game.

1897 Voorhees Normal and Industrial School, founded at Denmark by Elizabeth Evelyn Wright, was named for benefactor Ralph Voorhees.

General Hospital was established in Columbia.

Dr. Matilda Arabelle Evans, who graduated from the Women's Medical College of Pennsylvania that year, established the first black hospital in Columbia. She became the first female physician in Columbia and the first South Carolina black woman to practice medicine in the state.

The first volume of Edward McCrady's four volume history of South Carolina was published.

February 25. Bamberg, Cherokee, and Dorchester counties were organized.

March 2. Greenwood County was created from parts of Abbeville and Edgefield counties.

March 5. Legislation providing for a state income tax was enacted.

1898 *February 19.* The legislature passed a law, in the spirit of *Plessy* v. *Ferguson,* that separate coaches for whites and blacks were required on all railroads operating in South Carolina.

April 25. War was declared on Spain. Many South Carolinians volunteered for service in the Spanish-American War.

May 3. Septima Poinsette Clark, educator and civil rights leader, was born.

November 8. The state's last election day riot took place in Phoenix, in Greenwood County, and resulted in the deaths of one white and seven black persons.

December 5. Civil rights leader Modjeska Montieth Simkins was born in Columbia.

1899 Writer and women's suffrage advocate Virginia Durant Young became sole owner of the *Fairfax Enterprise.*

The company that would evolve into Sonoco Products was established at Hartsville to manufacture paper cones used in the growing textile industry.

1900 **U.S. Census**

White	557,807
Black	782,321
Other	188
Total	1,340,316

September 29–October 2. Race riots in Georgetown ended the Reconstruction practice of having a "fusion" ticket whereby political offices were divided between blacks and whites. The system of fusion had lasted longer in Georgetown than anywhere else in the state.

November. William McKinley was reelected president. South Carolina cast nine electoral votes for William Jennings Bryan.

1901 *February 4.* The South Carolina Bar Association was reestablished after a ten year hiatus.

December 1–May 31, 1902. The Interstate and West Indian Exposition was held in Charleston.

1902 *February 22.* In the U.S. Senate chamber, Tillman assaulted the state's moderate and progressive Senator John L. McLaurin.

February 25. Lee County was created from Darlington, Kershaw, and Sumter counties.

April 11. Wade Hampton died.

1903 *January 5.* Theodore Roosevelt appointed a black, Dr. William D. Crum, collector of the Port of Charleston.

January 15. N. G. Gonzales, editor of *The State,* was shot and killed by Lieutenant Governor James H. Tillman, nephew of Ben Tillman. A Lexington County jury (after a change of venue) found Tillman not guilty.

February 13. The state's first child labor law, introduced by Richland County Senator J. Q. Marshall, passed the legislature. As of May 1, 1903, no child under ten years of age could be employed in a factory, mine, or mill in the state. As of May 1, 1904, it would be eleven years, and as of May 1, 1905, twelve years of age.

June 6. A great flood on the Pacolet River took over sixty lives.

1904 Lander Academy for women, a Methodist institution, was moved from Williamston to Greenwood and renamed Lander College. In 1951 Greenwood County assumed operation of the school and on July 1, 1973, Lander became a state supported college.

November. Theodore Roosevelt was elected president. South Carolina cast nine electoral votes for Alton B. Parker.

1905 Gibbes Art Gallery, built with a bequest by Charleston merchant James S. Gibbes, opened.

Bernard Baruch recreated Hobcaw Barony.

1907 *February 16.* The corrupt and controversial state Dispensary system was abolished.

February 19. An act to provide full secondary education throughout the state was passed.

1908 Uly Brooks published the first volume of his projected two-volume *South Carolina Bench and Bar.*

Electrocution superceded hanging as the state's mode of execution.

The initial subscription was made for Coker College for women in Hartsville.

February 14. Calhoun County was created from parts of Orangeburg and Lexington counties.

November. William H. Taft was elected president. South Carolina cast nine electoral votes for William Jennings Bryan.

November 3. Ellison Durant ("Cotton Ed") Smith was elected to the U.S. Senate, where he continued to sit until his death on November 17, 1944.

1910 **U.S. Census**

White	679,161
Black	833,843
Other	396
Total	1,515,400

The South Carolina Federation of Colored Women's Clubs was organized.

February 5. Dillon County was created from Marion County.

February 26. The State Board of Law Examiners was created.

November 8. Coleman L. ("Coley") Blease was elected governor on a platform of extreme race hatred and disgust with the white gentry.

1911 *February 11.* Henry Timrod's "Carolina" was adopted as the state song.

August 27. A severe hurricane wiped out the last attempts to grow rice commercially in the state.

1912 *January 30.* Jasper County was created from parts of Beaufort and Hampton counties.

November. Woodrow Wilson was elected president. South Carolina cast nine electoral votes for him.

1914 David R. Coker founded the Coker Pedigree Seed Company.

In Columbia, "The University Press" (later called the University of South Carolina Press) began publishing scholarly monographs.

Blease failed to unseat Senator "Cotton Ed" Smith in the Democratic state primary.

April. Jane Bruce Guignard led Columbia's suffragettes.

July. A wildcat strike at Lewis Parker's Monaghan Mill in Greenville erupted into a major confrontation. The workers were organized by the Industrial Workers of the World.

August 3. Germany declared war on France.

1915   *February 20.* The State Tax Commission was established.

February 20. The state's first compulsory education bill passed. It became effective July 1, 1915, and applied to children eight to fourteen years of age.

February 20. Under the new governor, Richard I. Manning, modern social-welfare legislation in South Carolina began with the establishment of the State Board of Charities and Corrections.

In a referendum, South Carolina voted to prohibit the sale of all alcoholic beverages (see 1933).

October 21. The film *Birth of a Nation,* a portrayal of Reconstruction in South Carolina, premiered in the state.

1916   *January.* The first Anderson car was built at Rock Hill by John Gary Anderson. Although this was the South's most successful car, the firm went bankrupt within a decade.

February 19. McCormick County was created from portions of Abbeville, Edgefield, and Greenwood counties.

February 29. A Child Labor Law raised the minimum age for employment to fourteen.

July 11. President Wilson signed the Federal Road Act.

July. The great flood of 1916 swept down from the mountains of North Carolina and was especially destructive in the Pee Dee.

1917   The boll weevil was first detected in South Carolina.

February 20. The State Highway Department was established. Henceforth, licenses were required for all motor vehicles. The state took responsibility for a state road system.

February 27. The first South Carolina chapter of the NAACP was founded at Charleston with portrait painter and businessman Edwin A. Harleston as its president.

April 6. The U.S. entered World War I and Governor Manning appointed a Commission on Civic Preparedness for War (chairman David R. Coker). Shortly thereafter National Guard camps were established outside Greenville and Spartanburg and a U.S. Army camp was located near Columbia. The navy yard near Charleston was expanded.

July 18. The U.S. Army camp on former Hampton property on the eastern edge of Columbia was named Camp Jackson by the War Department, in honor of Andrew Jackson. (See 1940.)

October 21. Jazz trumpeter "Dizzy" Gillespie was born in Cheraw.

1918   *February 14.* Legislation permitted women to practice law in the state. James M. "Miss Jim" Perry became the first South Carolina woman admitted to the Bar.

June 25. James Lide Coker, who had done much to aid agriculture by seed testing and plant development, died.

July 3. Benjamin R. Tillman died.

September 30. Women were admitted to the College of Charleston.

October. An influenza epidemic, which reached its height with 4,274 deaths that month, resulted in 170,000 cases and 7,400 deaths in South Carolina.

November 11. The Armistice which ended World War I was signed. 62,000 South Carolinians had served during the conflict.

1919   The boll weevil destroyed 90 percent of the Sea Island cotton crop. Cotton was never again grown successfully on a commercial scale in the Sea Islands.

January. A black convention at Columbia, with representatives from across the state, complained about segregation and voting restrictions, and called for better education and representation on school boards.

February 6. Allendale County was created from Barnwell and Hampton counties.

June 9. Petigru, the first law school building on the University of South Carolina campus, was dedicated.

October 9. Town Theater, the oldest surviving community theater in the country, offered its first productions—"Joint Owners in Spain" and "The Rising of the Moon"—in the Columbia High School auditorium.

1920 U.S. Census

White	818,538
Black	864,719
Other	467
Total	1,683,724

April 21. Community leaders held the first meeting to organize the Society for the Preservation of Old Dwellings in Charleston.

September. Black teachers replaced white teachers in Charleston black public schools in response to an NAACP-organized campaign.

Women voted for first time in the state after the adoption of the Nineteenth Amendment (August 26, 1920). South Carolina, however, did not ratify the amendment until 1969.

November 2. Warren G. Harding was elected president. South Carolina cast nine electoral votes for James Cox.

1921 A long agricultural depression began.

In Charleston, the Poetry Society published its first yearbook.

Wil Lou Gray helped launch the Opportunity School as an adult education program.

August 3. "Shoeless" Joe Jackson of Greenville was banned from professional baseball by Judge

Kenesaw Mountain Landis for his alleged participation in the 1919 "Black Sox" scandal.

1922 Lucile Ellerbe Godbold won an Olympic gold
medal. She was the first woman named to the
South Carolina Athletic Hall of Fame.

March 15. A law was passed limiting the hours of
work in textile mills to ten hours a day or fifty-five
hours a week.

1923 For the first time in over a century whites out-
numbered blacks in South Carolina. The proportion of blacks had declined following 1880, with
their increasing emigration to the North and Mid-
west.

May 17. A fire at Cleveland School, near Camden,
claimed seventy lives, including that of the father
of the future governor John West.

October 29. "Runnin' Wild" opened on Broadway,
introducing the dance known as "The Charleston."

1924 *March 21.* The "6–0–1" school law was passed: the
state would pay a teacher's salary for six months
if the county would pay for one month.

February 1. The yellow jessamine (*Gelsemium
sempervirens*) was adopted as the state flower.

November 4. Calvin Coolidge was elected president. South Carolina cast nine electoral votes for
John W. Davis.

1926 The development of Myrtle Beach as a resort began with John T. Woodside's Ocean Forest Hotel.

1927 *April 26.* The State Forestry Commission was established.

1928 *June 28.* The Congaree River (Gervais Street) Bridge, connecting Columbia and West Columbia, was opened to traffic.

November 6. Mrs. Mary Gordon Ellis was elected senator for Jasper County, the first woman elected to the South Carolina legislature.

November 6. Herbert Hoover was elected president. South Carolina cast nine electoral votes for Alfred E. Smith.

1929 The South Carolina Legislature held hearings on labor conditions and concluded that textile workers had valid complaints against management.

March 14. The legislature authorized an unprecedented $65 million bond issue, of doubtful constitutionality, to complete the state highway system.

May 24. Julia Peterkin's novel *Scarlet Sister Mary* won the Pulitzer Prize.

August 8. The Cooper River Bridge, joining Charleston and Mount Pleasant, was opened to traffic. The two-mile-long bridge (with a main span of 1,050 feet and a vertical clearance of 150 feet) was one of the longest highway bridges in the world.

September 20. Columbia's Owens Field opened to commercial passengers.

October 29. In New York, prices collapsed on the New York Stock Exchange.

1930 U.S. Census

White	944,049
Black	793,681
Other	1,035
Total	1,738,765

April. The first driver's licenses were issued and the state highway patrol was established.

May 9. WCSC, a Charleston radio station, initiated the first broadcast in the state.

July. Electric power was generated from the Dreher Shoals Dam on the Saluda River in Lexington County. It was then the largest earthen dam in the world for hydroelectricity. Lake Murray gradually formed behind it.

November 4. James F. Byrnes defeated "Coley" Blease for the U.S. Senate. Byrnes, who became the state's most influential representative in Washington since Calhoun, sat in the U.S. Senate until he was appointed to the U.S. Supreme Court.

1931 Sculptor Anna Vaughan Hyatt Huntington and her husband Archer Milton Huntington founded Brookgreen Gardens near Georgetown.

October 13. The Charleston City Council passed the nation's first Historic Preservation ordinance.

December 31. The failure of People's State Bank began a run on other banks.

1932 *November 8.* Franklin D. Roosevelt was elected president. South Carolina cast eight electoral votes for him. (He received almost 98 percent of the state's popular vote.)

A constitutional amendment, implemented by legislation the following year, changed South Carolina's fiscal year from January 1–December 31 to July 1–June 30.

1933 *December 5.* The Twenty-first Amendment repealed the Eighteenth Amendment and ended national prohibition. South Carolina, however, legalized only beer and wine, still forbidding the sale of strong liquors under the 1915 laws (see 1935).

1934 The U.S. Soil Erosion Service began planting kudzu in Spartanburg County.

May 19. Governor Ibra C. Blackwood signed the act which created the South Carolina Public Service Authority, which was to build the Santee-Cooper dams.

September 1–22. About 45,000 of the state's 80,000 textile workers actively participated in the United Textile Workers (A. F. of L.) strike. Seven workers were shot and killed by special deputies at Chiquola Mills at Honea Path.

1935 David Duncan Wallace's *History of South Carolina* was completed with the publication of the final two volumes of the four volume work.

May 14. With the end of national prohibition, South Carolina passed an alcoholic beverage control law to regulate the sale of liquor.

October 10. George Gershwin's opera *Porgy and Bess,* with words by Ira Gershwin based on Du-

Bose Heyward's novel *Porgy,* received its first performance at the Alvin Theater in New York City.

October 28. A constitutional crisis arose when Governor Olin D. Johnston proclaimed the State Highway Department in rebellion and ordered the National Guard to occupy its offices. No irregularities were found in the operations of the department, which ran itself with exemplary efficiency but which was politically independent and insensitive.

1936 *May.* Appointment of highway commissioners was placed in the hands of the legislature (previously the commissioners had been appointed by the governor for staggered terms).

June 25. Senator "Cotton Ed" Smith walked out of the Democratic National Convention in protest when a black clergyman was selected to offer an invocation.

November 3. Franklin D. Roosevelt was reelected president. South Carolina cast eight electoral votes for him.

1937 *February 24.* The South Caroliniana Society held its first annual meeting in Columbia.

May 13. The South Carolina Public Welfare Act was passed to implement the national Social Security Act, providing aid for the blind, aged, and handicapped.

August 1. A Columbia widow received the first Social Security check delivered in South Carolina.

November 26. The new Dock Street Theatre, constructed on the site of the original playhouse, with a combination of local and WPA funds, opened with a performance of "The Recruiting Officer."

December 12. A riot at the state penitentiary in Columbia left one officer dead. Six inmates were convicted in the death and all were executed March 24, 1939.

1938 *March 12.* The State Planning Board was established. It evolved into the State Development Board.

June 14–August 30. The most colorful primary in the history of the state pitted "Cotton Ed" Smith, Olin D. Johnston, and Edgar Brown against each other for the U.S. Senate. Smith won.

September 20. Twenty-nine persons were killed when two tornadoes struck Charleston.

November 8. Burnet Maybank became the first Charlestonian since the Civil War to be elected governor.

1939 *January 28.* The "air cooled" Riviera Theater opened in Charleston.

March 17. The palmetto was officially adopted as the state tree.

April 18. The clearing of land for the Santee-Cooper dams and powerhouses began.

September 1. In Europe, World War II began with the German invasion of Poland.

1940 **U.S. Census**

White	1,084,308
Black	814,164
Other	1,332
Total	1,899,804

June. The reactivated Camp Jackson became Fort Jackson, a permanent army post.

August 11. About forty persons were killed in a hurricane that tore through Beaufort, Edisto Island, and Charleston.

November 5. Franklin D. Roosevelt was reelected president. South Carolina cast eight electoral votes for him.

1941 In New York, Wilbur J. Cash's *The Mind of the South* was published.

March 17. David Edward Finley, of York, oversaw the opening of the National Gallery of Art as its first director.

July 7. James F. Byrnes took his oath as an associate justice of the U.S. Supreme Court.

December 11. Cassandra Maxwell of Orangeburg became the first black woman admitted to the South Carolina Bar.

1942 Annie Greene Nelson published her first novel, *After the Storm.*

March 5. The State Ports Authority was established.

April 18. General Jimmy Doolittle led a squadron of B-25s, made up of crews from the Columbia Army Air Base, in a bombing raid on Tokyo. Veterans of the raid assembled in Columbia in 1992 to mark the fiftieth anniversary of the event.

October. James F. Byrnes resigned from the U.S. Supreme Court to become director of economic stabilization.

December 2. The Santee-Cooper project was substantially complete.

1943 *May 27.* President Roosevelt named James F. Byrnes director of war mobilization. Byrnes acquired the reputation of being "assistant president."

1944 The Progressive Democratic Party was organized by blacks to encourage political activity in the black community and to pressure the state Democratic Party to admit black members.

The U.S. Supreme Court, in the *Smith* v. *Allwright* decision, ruled the white-only Democratic Party illegal for denying black citizens the right to vote in primary elections.

The University of South Carolina Press was reorganized as a separate department of the University of South Carolina.

April 14. Governor Olin D. Johnston called a special session of the General Assembly to separate party primaries from state control. The legislature responded by enacting 147 laws in six days to exclude black voters by allowing political parties to hold primaries as private organizations.

July 19–20. Byrnes was overlooked as the Democratic vice presidential nominee because of opposition from labor and black leaders.

November 7. Franklin D. Roosevelt was reelected president. South Carolina cast eight electoral votes for him.

1945 *August.* World War II ended. Over 170,000 South Carolinians served during the war.

1946 *November 4.* Strom Thurmond was elected governor.

1947 *February 16.* A mob seized Willie Earle from the Pickens County jail and murdered him. This was the last lynching in the state. Thirty-one defendants were acquitted in a highly publicized Greenville trial.

July 12. Judge Waites Waring issued his decision in *Elmore* v. *Rice* which brought an end to the all-white Democratic primary.

1948 The eighteen-story Cornell Arms apartment building in Columbia became the state's first "skyscraper."

July 17. Dissident Southern Democrats or "Dixiecrats" convened in Birmingham where they nominated Strom Thurmond as the presidential candidate of their States' Rights Party.

November 2. Strom Thurmond was defeated, running a distant third behind Harry Truman, carrying only four Southern states and thirty-nine electoral votes, including South Carolina's eight.

December 6. The Greenville Symphony gave its first performance.

1949   *April 4.* Marian Anderson performed before a segregated audience at the Columbia Township Auditorium.

April 15. The legislature ratified a state constitutional amendment that permitted divorce on the grounds of adultery, desertion, physical cruelty, or habitual drunkenness; previously divorce was not granted on any grounds.

October. David Edward Finley founded the National Trust for Historic Preservation.

November 11. Black parents with the assistance of the NAACP charged the segregated Clarendon County school system discriminated against their children. Their suit eventually became part of the *Brown* v. *Board of Education of Topeka* case.

1950   **U.S. Census**

White	1,293,405
Black	822,077
Other	1,545
Total	2,117,027

The State Budget and Control Board replaced the Budget Commission. Under a reorganization plan adopted by the Assembly, ten state agencies were abolished and their functions and duties were assumed by the Budget and Control Board.

The Dupont Corporation opened the May chemical plant in Camden.

March. The Columbia Museum of Art opened.

April 15. A new law school building was dedicated at the University of South Carolina—the "second" Petigru.

November 28. The Atomic Energy Commission and Dupont selected a 250,000 acre site in Aiken and Barnwell counties for the Savannah River plant. It was created to produce plutonium and tritium, elements used in nuclear weapons. The facility would become one of the largest employers in the state, but also a focal point for antinuclear power protestors and environmental activists.

1951   *March 12.* The South Carolina Philharmonic Orchestra gave its first performance.

April 15. Governor Byrnes instituted a $75 million program to make black schools as good as white schools. A 3 percent sales tax, the first in the history of the state, was levied to finance the program.

1952   *November 4.* Voters approved an amendment to the state constitution empowering the legislature to close public schools if necessary to avoid integration.

November 4. Dwight Eisenhower was elected president. South Carolina cast eight electoral votes for Adlai Stevenson.

1953   *June 19.* The state's first television station—WCSC, Charleston—began broadcasting.

November 7. Columbia's first television station went on the air.

1954 *March 19.* "Right to Work" legislation was passed outlawing the closed shop.

May 17. The U.S. Supreme Court, in *Brown* v. *Board of Education of Topeka,* ruled that "separate but equal" schools were unconstitutional.

November 2. Strom Thurmond was elected to the U.S. Senate on a write-in vote, defeating the regular candidate of the Democratic Party, State Senator Edgar Brown.

1955 *May 18.* Mary McLeod Bethune, founder and president of Bethune Cookman College and former director of the Division of Negro Affairs of the National Youth Administration, died at Daytona Beach, Florida.

1956 *January 10–April 10.* The General Assembly, in its "segregation session," passed laws to avoid integration by circumventing recent Supreme Court rulings.

November 6. Dwight Eisenhower was reelected president. South Carolina cast eight electoral votes for Adlai Stevenson.

1957 Marian McKnight reigned as South Carolina's only "Miss America."

Althea Gibson became the first South Carolinian as well as the first black to compete at Wimbledon and, in 1958, the only black woman to win the Wimbledon title.

1958 *January.* Jasper Johns' one-man exhibition at Leo Castelli's New York Gallery helped launch the Pop Art movement.

September. Experimental classroom use of television at Columbia's Dreher High School led to the establishment of South Carolina Educational Television (SCETV) in 1960.

1959 *October 22.* Clemson defeated the University of South Carolina, 27–0, in the last Big Thursday football game.

1960 **U.S. Census**

White	1,551,022
Black	829,291
American Indian	1,098
Japanese	460
Chinese	158
Filipino	328
Other	237
Total	2,382,594

January 1. The first modern civil rights demonstration in South Carolina took place when blacks marched to the Greenville airport to protest the segregated waiting rooms. The march had been provoked when baseball star Jackie Robinson was insulted and threatened with arrest for entering the "white" waiting room.

February 12. The term "sit-in" began to be used when about 100 black students from Friendship Junior College in Rock Hill entered two of the city's largest variety stores and requested service at the lunch counters.

November 8. John F. Kennedy was elected president. South Carolina cast eight electoral votes for him.

1961 *February 6.* Students refused to pay fines and asked for jail sentences in Rock Hill. This was a "jail-in."

March 2. Civil rights advocates staged an anti-segregation march on the state capitol in Columbia.

May 15. The state launched its technical education program.

1962 *March 15.* The Senate adopted a concurrent resolution that had originated in the House February 14, requesting that the Confederate flag be "flown on the flagpole on top of the State House."

March 17. The Fifteenth Judicial District was formed by taking Georgetown and Horry Counties from the Twelfth Circuit.

October 24. Parr Shoals, the state's first nuclear power plant, was dedicated.

November 6. William D. Workman, Jr.'s senatorial campaign against Olin D. Johnston ended in defeat but it demonstrated a new vitality in the South Carolina Republican Party.

1963 *January 16.* Governor Donald S. Russell's inaugural barbecue was the first integrated public social event since Reconstruction.

January 28. Harvey Gantt was the first black to enroll as a student at Clemson College.

September. The first black students in the modern era were admitted to the University of South Carolina.

1964 *Who Speaks for the South?* by James McBride Dabbs was published in New York.

Baptist College was established at Charleston. The institution's name was changed to Charleston Southern in 1990.

July 2. The Federal Civil Rights Act, outlawing race, gender, religious, or ethnic-based discrimination in public accommodations and employment, became law.

September 16. Senator Strom Thurmond left the Democratic Party and joined the Republican Party.

October 29. The Nobel Prize in Physics was awarded to South Carolinian Charles Townes of Greenville.

November 3. Lyndon Johnson was elected president. However, Barry Goldwater became the first Republican presidential candidate to carry South Carolina (eight electoral votes) since the end of Reconstruction.

VII. THE MODERN STATE
(1965–1992)

By the time the state came to celebrate its 300th birthday in 1970, the unforgettable performances in Charleston of *Porgy and Bess,* in which blacks and whites worked and watched side by side as equals without any self-consciousness, suggested that the state had finally found the goal which had been working itself out. With just enough of the old bravura and self-confidence to prevent dullness, South Carolina now seems ready at last to offer modesty, sanity, and thoughtfulness to a world in dire need of such qualities.

1965   Furman University admitted Joseph A. Vaughn and became the state's first private white institution of higher education to integrate.

August 6. The Federal Voting Rights Act became law ending all barriers to black voter registration.

1966   *March 29.* The Sixteenth Judicial Circuit was formed of York and Union counties.

1967   *March 1.* An amendment to the state constitution opened the way for women to serve on juries in state courts.

March 30. The State Department of Parks, Recreation, and Tourism was established.

June 20. A "Brown Bag" law was passed at the instance of the growing state tourism industry.

One could carry a liquor bottle into a restaurant in a brown paper bag.

1968 Moody's, a New York investment firm, was commissioned by the governor's office to rate South Carolina's institutions and government. The report concluded that improvement in education should be the highest priority.

February 8. Three black students at South Carolina State College in Orangeburg were killed in a riot. Students at the predominantly black college had been protesting against the refusal of the white owner of a bowling alley to admit black students.

March 4. "Smokin' Joe" Frazier of Beaufort County won the World Heavyweight boxing championship.

March 14. With the establishment of the State Bar, membership by all lawyers was mandatory.

July. South Carolina's delegation to the turbulent Democratic National Convention at Chicago was integrated and as such was the only Southern state delegation that went unchallenged.

October 16. Fort Jackson was incorporated into the city of Columbia. The resulting area of the city was eighty-two square miles.

November 5. Richard Nixon was elected president. South Carolina cast eight electoral votes for him.

1969 Interstate highway 26, linking the mountains to the coast, was completed.

November 21. Clement Haynsworth's nomination to the U.S. Supreme Court by President Nixon was rejected by the U.S. Senate.

1970 U.S. Census

White	1,794,430
Black	789,041
Native American	2,241
Filipino	1,222
Japanese	826
Chinese	521
Other	2,235
Total	2,590,516

Columbia was first South Carolina city to exceed 100,000 in population.

May 7. Antiwar demonstrations at the University of South Carolina escalated into a takeover of the administration building, during which the National Guard was called to restore order.

June 25. Gershwin's *Porgy and Bess* (see 1935, October 10) was performed in South Carolina for the first time. As part of the state's Tricentennial celebrations, fourteen performances were given before integrated audiences in the Charleston Municipal Auditorium. The performances were presented by the Charleston Symphony Association and underwritten by the Tricentennial Commission.

Republican Congressman Albert Watson ran for governor in the last racially oriented statewide campaign and was defeated by John West.

November 3. Herbert U. Fielding of Charleston, and James L. Felder and I. S. Leevy Johnson of Columbia became the first black members of the South Carolina General Assembly since 1895.

1970–1971 South Carolina public schools were desegregated under federal court order. School districts throughout the state merged the former dual black-white schools into unitary districts.

1971 *October.* The first integrated State Fair opened.

November. The Bar Foundation was created to raise funds to improve the education of lawyers.

1972 Pat Conroy's *The Water is Wide* was published. This was the first of four of his novels to become a motion picture.

April 9. James F. Byrnes died.

November 7. The people of the state approved a constitutional amendment to revise the South Carolina judicial system.

November 7. Richard Nixon was reelected president. South Carolina cast eight electoral votes for him.

1973 *February 9.* The state's heaviest snowfall was recorded, from 24 inches in the central part of the state to 9 inches in Charleston.

February 11. The South Carolina Hall of Fame was founded at Myrtle Beach. Astronaut Colonel Charles M. Duke, Jr., became the first inductee.

March 29. South Carolina restaurants served the first legal mixed drinks in the state. The "brown bag" era was brought to a close by a constitutional amendment which passed in November 1972 and was ratified by the legislature on March 28, 1973.

April 4. The legislature passed an act to implement the constitutional provision for judicial reform.

July 1. William A. Dallis became the first South Carolina Court Administrator.

July 6. Adjournment of the 100th General Assembly marked the last South Carolina legislature elected by counties. The U.S. Supreme Court had ruled June 25, 1973, in *Stevenson* v. *West,* that legislative districts coinciding with county or other political boundaries violated the principle of "one man, one vote." The state was reapportioned according to population.

1974 *February 15.* Kiawah Island was purchased from C. C. Royal by a corporate subsidiary of the Kuwait Sheikdom, to develop as a resort.

May 2–4. A celebration was held to dedicate the new Law Center at the University of South Carolina.

June 25. The Local Government Act provided counties more local control.

September 23. Charles D. "Pug" Ravenel, the Democratic nominee for governor, was disqualified for not meeting the five-year residence requirement.

November 5. The election of Governor James B. Edwards marked the rise of the modern Republican Party in the state and with it the return of the two-party system.

November 5. Juanita W. Goggins, of York County, became the first black woman elected to the state legislature.

1975 *January 31.* The South Carolina Bar Association voted in favor of ending its existence. Members of that organization joined members of the State Bar to form the South Carolina Bar.

October 13. The National Naval and Maritime Museum was dedicated at Patriots Point where the USS *Yorktown* is permanently anchored.

December 9. Joseph P. Riley, Jr., was elected mayor of Charleston.

1976 *August 5.* Thomas A. Yawkey, sportsman and conservationist, bequeathed 15,000 acres and $10 million to maintain a game preserve and wilderness area in Georgetown County.

October 18. Congress enacted legislation to establish the Congaree Swamp National Monument.

November 2. Jimmy Carter was elected president. South Carolina cast eight electoral votes for Gerald Ford.

1977 *May.* The first Spoleto Festival was held at Charleston.

June 8. Governor James B. Edwards signed the legislation which reestablished the death penalty.

June 10. The Education Finance Act was passed to establish an equitable basis for the distribution of public education funds.

September 19. The U.S. Interior Department ruled that the Catawba Indians possessed a valid claim to 144,000 acres in York and Lancaster counties including the cities of Rock Hill and Fort Mill.

October 22. Prince Charles, heir to the British throne, visited Charleston for the first time.

1978 *November 7.* Nancy Stevenson's election as lieutenant governor marked the first election of a woman to a statewide office.
Janie Glymph Goree of Carlisle became the first black woman elected mayor in South Carolina.

1979 *April 23.* Michelin Tire announced that it would build a $100 million plant in Lexington County, adding to its investment in the state which included facilities at Anderson, Greenville, and Spartanburg.

September 22. Matthew J. Perry became the first black federal judge in the history of South Carolina.

November 19. South Carolina native Lane Kirkland was elected president of the AFL-CIO.

1980 **U.S. Census**

White	2,147,224
Black	948,623
Native American	5,665
Filipino	3,696

Asian Indian	2,152
Japanese	1,415
Chinese	1,404
Korean	1,390
Vietnamese	1,072
Hawaiian	439
Ghanian	189
Samoan	77
Eskimo	70
Aleut	22
Other	8,382
Total	3,121,820

April 19. The new Charleston Museum building opened.

July. Shawn Weatherly was selected "Miss Universe."

October 7. Congressman John Jenrette was convicted of accepting a $50,000 bribe from FBI agents masquerading as representatives of Arab sheiks seeking political favors.

October 28. The Governor's School for the Arts was established at Greenville.

October 28. Catawbas brought suit claiming title to 140,000 acres in Lancaster and York counties.

November 4. Ronald Reagan was elected president. South Carolina cast eight electoral votes for him.

Lee Atwater gained national prominence as the mastermind of Ronald Reagan's "southern strategy." His campaign strategy through the election of 1988 made Atwater one of the leading figures in the national Republican Party.

December 1. University of South Carolina football player George Rogers won the Heisman trophy.

1981 *October 5.* The Old Exchange Building in Charleston was rededicated after a $2 million renovation.

November 2. U.S. Customs officials made their first arrests in "Operation Jackpot" that uncovered international drug smuggling operations centered in South Carolina.

1982 *April.* Reuben Greenberg became Charleston's first black chief of police.

June 18. An agreement between a local environmental group that wished to protect the Santee-Cooper basin and the Union Camp corporation ended a year of negotiations. The paper mill was opened in Richland County in 1984.

1983 *January.* Filming of *The Big Chill* was completed in Beaufort. The movie opened in September and became the best-known production of the state's film industry.

February 2. South Carolina native Joseph Bernardin, the archbishop of Chicago, was consecrated a cardinal in the Catholic Church.

July 27. The legislature elected the members of the recently created six-judge Court of Appeals.

October 25. The Reverend I. DeQuincy Newman became the first black state senator in the twentieth century.

1984 *March 28.* Ten South Carolinians were killed when numerous tornadoes ravaged the state. Ronald Reagan declared four counties—Abbeville, Fairfield, Marlboro, and Newberry—disaster areas.

April 1. Georgetown celebrated its 250th anniversary.

July 27. The Reverend Daniel Joseph Jenkins (d. 1937) became the first black person to have his or her portrait approved for hanging in Charleston's City Hall. The portrait, unveiled February 28, 1985, was painted by Merton D. Simpson who was raised in Jenkins' orphanage.

May 26. The V. C. Summer Nuclear Station was dedicated at Jenkinsville after thirteen years of delays from legal and civic opposition.

November 6. Richard Riley became the state's first governor elected to consecutive four-year terms.

November 6. Ronald Reagan was elected president. South Carolina cast eight electoral votes for him.

December 31. The Education Improvement Act passed after Governor Richard Riley convinced the legislature to increase the state sales tax by one cent to raise $250 million a year for public schools.

1985 *January 16.* Retired Chief Justice Joseph Moss, serving as a special judge, was forced to leave the bench permanently after a furor over an alledged racial slur.

July 12. Ernest A. Finney, Jr. became the first black justice elected to the South Carolina Supreme Court since Reconstruction. He qualified on July 22, 1985.

1986 *January 22.* Mack Trucks announced it would build an assembly plant in Fairfield County.

January 28. Astronaut Ronald E. McNair, a Lake City native, was killed in the *Challenger* explosion.

October 27. The State-Record Company announced that it had been purchased by the Knight-Ridder Company, ending ninety-five years of ownership by the Hampton family.

November 4. Elizabeth Patterson became the first woman elected to U.S. House of Representatives from South Carolina.

1987 *March 19.* Jim Bakker, television evangelist, resigned and brought on the collapse of the PTL (Praise the Lord) religious empire centered in York County.

September 11. Pope John Paul II visited Columbia.

1988 *January 27.* Jean H. Toal became first woman elected to the South Carolina Supreme Court. She qualified on March 17, 1988.

April 1. The *Columbia Record* ceased publication after ninety-one years.

June 7. The Beachfront Management Act was passed to control coastal development.

August 28. The Governor's School for Science and Mathematics opened to its first class on the campus of Coker College in Hartsville.

October 29. The State Museum opened in Columbia.

November 8. George Bush was elected president. South Carolina cast eight electoral votes for him.

1989 *January 14.* The Koger Center for the Arts in Columbia opened with a performance by the London Philharmonic Orchestra.

September 21–22. Hurricane Hugo. The storm surge reached nineteen feet above mean high tide at Awendah, north of Mount Pleasant.

October 11. FBI agents obtained the cooperation of lobbyist Ron Cobb and launched an investigation of corruption in the state legislature. Designated as Operation Lost Trust, the investigation resulted in numerous indictments and convictions over the next two years.

1990 **U.S. Census**

White	2,406,974
Black	1,039,884
Native Americans	8,049
Eskimo	106
Aleut	91
Chinese	3,039
Filipino	5,521
Japanese	1,885
Asian Indian	3,900
Korean	2,577
Vietnamese	1,752
Cambodian	239
Hmong	76
Laotian	598

Thai	565
Other Asian	1,247
Hawaiian	426
Samoan	159
Guamanian	317
Other Pacific Islanders	81
Others	9,217
Total	3,486,703

In the 1990 Census, 30,551 South Carolinians identified themselves as being of "Hispanic Origin."

May 30. University of South Carolina President James B. Holderman resigned in the face of increasing criticism and controversy.

June 12. Democrats nominated Theo Mitchell, a black Greenville legislator, as their candidate for governor.

August 24. The first indictments were handed down in the Operation Lost Trust investigation.

October 1. Charles P. Austin was sworn into office as Columbia's first black chief of police.

December 1. The Peace Center for the Performing Arts opened in Greenville.

1991 *March 29.* Lee Atwater died.

December. South Carolina National Bank, the state's oldest and largest bank, merged with Wachovia Bank of Winston-Salem, North Carolina, culminating a series of mergers and acquisitions that witnessed a general consolidation of the state's banks.

1992 *June.* BMW (Bayerische Motoren Werke) announced that it would build its first automobile factory outside Germany in Greenville County.

August. The Catawba Indians, after negotiations with state and federal officials, accepted $50 million in a preliminary agreement to settle their land dispute.

November 3. James Clyburn became the first African American elected to the U.S. Congress from South Carolina in the twentieth century.

November 3. Bill Clinton was elected president. South Carolina cast eight electoral votes for George Bush.

November 3. Maggie Glover, of Florence County, became the first African-American woman elected to the state senate.

December 21. Former Governor Richard Riley was selected by President-elect Bill Clinton to serve as secretary of education in the new administration.

INDEX

Abbeville, 102
Abbeville County, 59, 117, 122, 150
Abolitionists, 81, 85, 92
Acadians, 33
Active (sloop), 41
Act of Union (1707), 17
Adams, John, 57, 65, 67
Adams, John Quincy, 78
Adams, Mattie Jean, 114
Additional Instruction from George III, 44
"An Address to the People of South Carolina" (Turnbull), 83
"An Address to the States of the Union" (Calhoun and McDuffie), 83
AFL-CIO, 147
African Americans: as gubernatorial candidate, 153; on bench, 147, 150; disenfranchisement of, 110; education, 81, 84, 98, 115–116, 125, 141, 144; first woman admitted to the Bar, 132; honored, 150; in law enforcement, 149, 153; in legislature, 144, 146, 149, 154; in sports, 137, 142, 149; in U.S. House of Representatives, 106, 154; laws concerning, 70, 77–78, 84, 95, 102, 103; political organizations, 133; serve in Union Army, 99; status under the Constitution, 75; vote for first time, 104; *see also* Slaves
African Methodist Episcopal Church, 101

After the Storm (Nelson), 132
Agricultural Society of South Carolina, 59
Aiken, D. Wyatt, 105
Aiken County, 19, 106, 107, 136
Air-conditioning, 116; *see also* Riviera Theater
Aix-la-Chapelle, Treaty of, 31
Albemarle (ship), 7
Albemarle County, 13
Albemarle Point, 10, 11
Albemarle Sound, 1, 5, 8
Algonquian tribes, 2
Allen, Sara Campbell, 113
Allendale County, 124
Allen University, 110
All Saints parish, 41
Alston, Joseph, 72
Alston, Theodosia Burr, 72
Altamaha River (Ga.), 21, 27, 37
Alvin Theater, 130
Amelia (brig), 82
American Colonization Society, 80
American Slavery As It Is (Weld), 86
Anderson, 147
Anderson, Hugh, 29
Anderson, John Gary, 122
Anderson, Marian, 135
Anderson, Robert, 39
Anderson, Maj. Robert, 97, 102
Anderson car, 122
Anderson County, 50, 79, 110
Anecdotes of the Revolutionary War in America (Garden), 76
Ann (ship), 42
Annapolis convention, 59
Anne, Queen, 15

Ansonborough, 86
Anti-tax association, 23
Apalachee Indians, 16
Appalachian Mountains, 1
Arbuthnot, Marriot, 52, 53
Archdale, John, 14
Arsenal Academy, 104
Arsenal and Guard House, 77
Articles of Confederation, 51,
    57, 59, 60
Artists, 17, 27, 123, 128
Ashley Cooper, Anthony (Baron
    Ashley of Wimborne St. Giles),
    5, 6, 11
Ashley Ferry Town, 35
Ashley River, 10, 11, 14, 32, 56
Assembly (first in colony), 10
Assembly, Commons House of,
    15; acts disallowed, 20;
    asserts authority, 23, 32, 36,
    40, 42–43, 44; on education,
    19; establishes religion, 17; on
    Indian slavery, 16; and Indian
    trade, 18; and interest laws,
    31; and proprietary rule, 21;
    speaker, 30
Assembly, S.C., 49; at
    Jacksonborough, 53, 54, 57;
    and labor legislation, 112;
    legislative districts changed,
    145; passes child labor law,
    119, 123; passes compulsory
    education law, 122; passes
    education laws, 126; and
    primary elections, 133; and
    segregation, 117, 137
Aston, Anthony, 16
Atomic Energy Commission, 136
Attakullakulla ("The Little
    Carpenter"), 34
Atwater, Lee, 148–149, 153
Audubon, John James, 82
Augusta (Ga.), 65
Austin, Charles P., 153
Avery Normal Institute, 103

Awendah, 152
Aztecs, 1

Bachman, John, 82
Backcountry, 39, 40, 42, 44, 46,
    47, 50, 54, 71
Bahamas (W.I.), 9, 22
Bakker, Jim, 151
Ball, John Coming, 54
Bamberg County, 117
Bank of Charleston, 84
Bank of South Carolina, 69
Bank of the State of South
    Carolina, 72
Bank of the United States, 65;
    Second, 75
Banks, 153; failure of, 128
Baptist College. *See* Charleston
    Southern University
Baptists, 12, 26, 88, 90, 106
Barbados (W.I.), 5, 6, 7; slaves
    from, 8
Bar Foundation, 144
Baring, Charles, 79
Barnwell, Col. John (Tuscarora
    Jack), 18, 19, 21, 22
Barnwell County, 59, 68, 124,
    136
Bartram, John, 34
Baruch, Bernard, 120
Beachfront Management Act,
    151
Beaufort, 9, 12, 43, 44, 73, 132;
    as capital, 38; Assembly called
    to meet in, 44; established, 18;
    incorporated, 70
Beaufort County, 108, 121
Beauregard, Gen. Pierre G.T.,
    97
Beecher, Henry Ward, 102
Bench and Bar (O'Neall), 93
Benedict Institute, 106
Bennett, W.J., 92
Berkeley, John (Baron Berkeley
    of Stratton), 5

Berkeley, Sir William, 5
Berkeley County, 12, 25, 42, 110
Bermuda, 9
Bernardin, Joseph, 149
Beth Elohim congregation, 31,
  65, 79
Bethune, Mary McLeod, 107,
  137
Bethune Cookman College, 137
The Big Chill, 149
"Big Thursday," 116–117, 138
Bill of Rights, 62
Bill of Rights, English, 13
Bills of credit, 16
Birth of a Nation, 122
Blackbeard. *See* Thatch (Teach),
  Edward
"Black Codes," 102, 103
Black Mingo Creek Bridge, 54
"Black Sox," 126
Blackstock's plantation, Battle
  of, 55
Blake, Daniel, 79
Blake, Edward, 49
Blanding, Abraham, 63
Blease, Coleman L. ("Coley"), 95,
  121, 128
Blind, school for the, 87
Blockades, 98
Bloody Marsh, Battle of, 29
Bluffton movement, 88
BMW (Bayerische Motoren
  Werke), 154
Board of Naval Commissioners,
  49
Board of Public Works, 74
Boll weevil, 123, 124
Bonham, Milledge L., 94, 99
Bonnet, Stede, 20, 21
Book of Common Prayer, 28
Boone, Thomas, 35, 36, 37
Botanists, 34
Boundaries, 6; commissions to
  survey, 25, 26
Bounties, 30

Bowman, John, 60
Bowman v. Middleton, 65
Brayne, Capt. Henry, 10
Breckinridge, John C., 96
British troops, 51, 52
Brookgreen Gardens, 128
Brooks, Preston, 92
Brooks, Uly, 120
Broughton Island packet (sloop),
  41
Brown, Edgar, 131, 137
"Brown Bag" law, 141, 145
Brown Fellowship Society, 62
*Brown v. Board of Education of
  Topeka*, 135, 137
Bryan, William Jennings, 116,
  118, 120
Buchanan, James, 92
Buford, Abraham, 53
Bull, Brig. Gen. Stephen, 51
Bull, Stephen, 10
Bull, William, II, 35, 45
Bulls Bay, 9, 17
Burr, Aaron, 65, 69
Burt, Armistead, 102
Bush, George, 152, 154
Butler, Andrew, 92
Butler, Pierce, 38, 39, 61
Butler, Pierce M., 89
Byrnes, James F., 115, 128, 132,
  133, 134, 136, 144

Cabot, John, 2
Cacique of Kiawah, 2, 10
Calhoun, John C., 57, 63, 111;
  as secretary of state, 87; as
  vice president, 79, 80, 83;
  death of, 90; first speech in
  Congress, 72; in Senate, 83,
  88, 90; marriage of, 72; and
  nullification, 81, 82, 83;
  secretary of war, 74; on
  slavery, 85; and states' rights,
  81, 83
Calhoun, Patrick, 34

Calhoun County, 120
Camden, 2, 3, 43, 44, 56, 65, 74, 79, 96, 126, 135
Camden, Battle of, 54
Campbell, Lt. Col. Archibald, 51
Campbell, Lord William, 36, 46, 47
Canby, Maj. Gen. E.R.S., 104, 105
Cape Fear, 8
Cape Fear River (N.C.), 6, 20
Cape Finisterre, Spain, 24
Capers, William, 81
Cardozo, Francis L., 103, 105
Carlisle, 147
Carolana, 5
Carolina, 7, 9
Carolina Coffee House, 75
Caroliniana Library, 87
Carter, Jimmy, 146
Carteret, Sir George, 5
Cash, E.B.C., 109
Cash, Wilbur J., 132
Cass, Lewis, 89
Castelli's New York Gallery, 137
Castle Pinckney, 66, 97
Catawba Indians, 37, 87, 147, 148, 154
Catesby, Mark, 22
Catholics, 65, 76, 149
Cedar Springs, 87
Central Correctional Institution, 104; *see also* State penitentiary
Challenger explosion, 151
Chamberlain, Daniel H., 107, 108
Chamber of Commerce, 59
Chapin, Sallie F., 109
Charles, Prince, 147
Charlesfort, 4
Charles II of England, 5
Charles I of England, 5
Charles IX of France, 4
Charleston (Charles Town, Charlestown), 4, 126; as walled city, 16; attempt to change name of, 22; attempt to incorporate, 22; branch of U.S. bank at, 65; British evacuation of, 57; celebrations at, 40; chief of police, 149; City Hall, 150; decline of, 71; earthquake at, 111; established, 11; evacuation of, 38; evolution of name, 38; fall of (1780), 38, 53; falls to Federal troops, 94, 101; fires in, 15, 27, 28–29, 50, 67, 84, 86, 98; growth of, 8, 9; hurricanes hit, 32; incorporation of, 58; Lafayette visits, 79; mobs in, 39; national Democratic Convention in, 96; navy yard, 123; preservation, 125, 128; religious disputes in, 28; schools at, 19, 92; slaves in, 22; Spoleto Festival, 146; state offices in, 78; tornadoes in, 131; Washington visits, 65
Charleston County, 110
Charleston Courier, 69–70
Charleston harbor, 47, 49, 81; fortifications in, 66; obstructed, 98
Charleston Homespun Company, 71
Charleston Insurance Company, 67
Charleston Library, 50
Charleston Mechanic Society, 66
Charleston Museum, 50, 148
Charleston Post and Courier, 70
Charleston Southern University, 140
Charleston Symphony Association, 143
Charleston Water Company, 68

Charlestown Chamber of
  Commerce, 45
Charles Town Library Society,
  31, 45
Charlestown Museum, 45
Cheraw, 43, 44, 79, 123
Cheraw Indians, 19
Cherokee, HMS, 47
Cherokee County, 117
Cherokee Indians, 20, 59;
  expeditions against, 34, 35,
  49; treaties with, 24, 34, 35,
  37, 50, 73
Chesnut, Mary Boykin, 96
Chester County, 59
Chesterfield County, 59
Cheves, Langdon, 73, 75, 90
Chickasaw Indians, 37
Chicora, 3
Chief Justices, 32, 48, 150
Choctaw Indians, 37
Cholera, 82, 85
Christ Church parish, 17
Church of England, 17, 28, 51;
  see also Episcopal Church
Churubusco, Battle of, 89
Cincinnati, Order of the, 58
Circuit Court Acts, 42, 43, 105
Circuit Court of Appeals,
  Federal, 111
The Citadel, 87, 97
City Tavern, 58
Civil Rights Acts, 116, 140
Civil Rights movement, 115–
  116; demonstrations, 138, 139,
  142
Claflin University, 105
Clarendon County, 92, 111, 135
Clarendon County (Cape Fear),
  6
Clark, Septima Poinsette, 117
Clay, Henry, 73
Clemson, Thomas G., 111
Clemson University, 111, 113,
  116, 117, 138, 139

Cleveland, Grover, 110, 111, 112,
  113
Cleveland School, 126
Clinton, Bill, 154
Clinton, Sir Henry, 49, 52, 53
Clyburn, James, 154
Cobb, Ron, 152
The Code of Honor (Wilson), 86
Coker, David R., 121, 123
Coker, James Lide, 85, 124
Coker College, 120, 151
Coker Pedigree Seed Company,
  121
Colhoun, Floride Bonneau, 72
College of Charleston, 58, 86,
  124
Colleton, James, 14
Colleton, Sir John, 5
Colleton County, 12, 18, 56, 68
Colonial agents, 32
Columbia: airports, 127; anti-
  segregation march on, 139;
  army camp, 123; as capital,
  39, 62; burned, 101; chief of
  police, 153; community
  theater in, 125; falls to federal
  troops, 101; first television
  station, 136; founding of, 60;
  General Hospital, 117;
  incorporated, 70; Lafayette
  visits, 79; Nullification in, 83;
  Sherman and, 94; size of, 142,
  143; state offices in, 78, 102;
  Washington visits, 65
Columbia Canal, 78
Columbia College, 93
Columbia Museum of Art, 136
Columbia Record, 151
Columbia Township Auditorium,
  135
Combahee Bluff, 57
Combahee River, 99
Commission on Civil
  Preparedness for War, 123
Common law of England, 19

Common Sense (Thomas Paine),
48
Compromise of 1808, 71
Compromise of 1850, 90
Conception (ship), 30
Concessions and Agreements, 6
Concord (Mass.), 46
Confederal Memorial
Association, 103
Confederate flag, 139
Confederate States of America,
97
Confitachiqui, 2, 3
Congaree Fort, 20
Congaree River, 56, 60, 104
Congaree River (Gervais Street)
Bridge, 127
Congarees, 42
Congaree Swamp National
Monument, 146
Congregational church, 11
Congress, U.S., 106, 146; *see
also* House of Representatives,
U.S.; Senate, U.S.
Conner, James, 96
Conroy, Pat, 144
Constitution, S.C. (1776), 48
Constitution, S.C. (1778), 50, 51
Constitution, S.C. (1790), 62, 65,
71, 72, 74, 100
Constitution, S.C. (1865), 102,
103
Constitution, S.C. (1868), 104
Constitution, S.C. (1895), 95,
113; amendments to, 135, 136,
141, 144, 145
Constitution, U.S., 39, 61, 62,
71, 75, 78; S.C. law violates,
84
Constitutional convention (U.S.),
61
Continental Army, Southern, 55
Continental Association, 46
Continental Congress: First, 45;
Second, 49, 50, 54–55, 57, 59

Convention of El Pardo, 27
Conventions: black, at
Columbia, 124; Democratic
national, 130, 142; for 1865
Constitution, 102; for 1868
Constitution, 104; for 1895
Constitution, 113; political,
96; Taxpayers, 106, 107
Converse, Dexter E., 103
Converse Manufacturing
Company, 103
Conyers, John Henry, 107
Coolidge, Calvin, 126
Cooper, Thomas, 75, 80, 84, 85
Cooperationists, 91
Cooper River, 11, 12, 15, 60, 65
Cooper River Bridge, 127
Cornell Arms, 134
Cornwallis, Gen. Charles, Lord,
53, 54
Cotton, 9, 69; first exports of,
66; impact of boll weevil on,
124; price of, 74, 82; sea
island, 62, 66; wealth from,
63, 75
Cotton gin, 66, 69
Council, S.C., 10, 13, 23, 32, 33,
37, 44
Council of Safety, 46
County Court Act, 59
County courts, 22
Courthouses, 78
Court of Appeals, 79, 149
Courts, 21, 28, 68, 113
Cowpens, Battle of, 55
Cox, James, 125
Craven, Charles, 19
Craven, William (Earl of
Craven), 5
Craven County, 12, 42
Creek Indians, 19, 20, 37
Cremation, 65
"The Crime against Kansas"
(Sumner), 92
"The Crisis" (Turnbull), 80

Crisp, Edward, 16
Crokatt, James, 32
Crop-lien system, 103
Crum, Dr. William D., 119
Cuming, Sir Alexander, 24
Cunningham, Ann Pamela, 92
Cusabo tribes, 2
Customs, collector of, 12, 41

Dabbs, James McBride, 140
Dallis, William A., 145
Dan River (Va.), 55
Darlington County, 59, 111, 113, 119
Daughters of the American Revolution, 112
David (submarine), 100
Davis, Jefferson, 100, 102
Davis, John W., 126
Deaf, school for the, 76, 87
de Avilés, Pedro Menéndez, 4
de Ayllón, Lucas Vásquez, 2, 3
Declaration of Independence, 49, 51
Declaration of Rights, 13
Declaratory Act, 40
Deerskins, 8
Defence (schooner), 47
Democratic Party, 115, 133, 134, 137, 153
Denmark, 117
De Soto, Hernando, 3, 4
d'Estaing, Comte de, 52
DeWitt's Corner, treaty of, 50
Dibble Plan, 110
Dillon County, 121
Dills Bluff, Battle of, 57
Discourse Concerning the deign'd Establishment of a New Colony to the South of Carolina . . . , A (Montgomery), 20
Dispensary system, 112, 113, 120
Divorce, 135

Dixiecrats, 134
Dock Street Theatre, 26, 131
Doolittle, Gen. Jimmy, 133
Dorchester, 14, 32, 56
Dorchester County, 117
Douglas, David, 29
Drayton, John, 27, 68
Drayton, William Henry, 47, 48, 49, 51
Drayton Hall, 27
Dreher High School, Columbia, 138
Dreher Shoals Dam, 128
Dueling, 35, 86, 109
Duke, Charles M., Jr., 144
Duke of Argyle, 36
DuPont, Gideon, 58
Du Pont, Adm. Samuel Francis, 99
Dupont Corporation, 135, 136

Earle, Willie, 134
Earthquakes, 111
Ebenezer (Ga.), 29
Edgefield, 94
Edgefield County, 116, 117, 122
Edict of Nantes, revocation of, 12
Edisto Island, 132
Edisto River, 57
Education, 120, 124, 139, 142; adult, 125; compulsory, 122; *see also* Schools
Education Finance Act, 147
Education Improvement Act, 150
Edwards, James B., 146
Ehrhardt, 101
"Eight Box Voting law," 110
Eisenhower, Dwight D., 136, 137
Elections: backcountry participation in, 42; disputed, 36, 108; first for African Americans, 104; laws concerning, 22; primary, 107,

Elections (*cont.*)
116, 121, 131, 133, 134; public, 10
Elkison v. *Deliesseline*, 78
Ellenton, 107
Elliott, William, 62
Ellis, Mary Gordon, 127
Elmore v. *Rice*, 134
Emancipation Day, 99
Emanuel African Methodist Episcopal Church, 77
Embargos, 71
Engineer, state, 74
England, John, 76
Epidemics, 27, 82, 85, 124
Episcopal Calvary Church, 89
Episcopal Church, 67
Erskine College, 86
Estatoe, 35
Etchohih, Battle of, 35
Eutaw Springs, Battle of, 56
Evans, Dr. Matilda Arabelle, 117
Eve, Abraham, 66
Exchange Building (Old Exchange), 41, 45, 68, 149
Executions, 21, 24, 47, 77, 120, 131; end of public, 109; made legal, 146
Exposition and Protest (Calhoun), 80

Fairfax Enterprise, 118
Fairfield County, 1, 59, 150, 151
FBI, 148, 152
Federalists, 39
Federal Road Act, 123
Felder, James L., 144
Fellowship Society, 43
Fence Law, 108
Ferguson, Maj. Patrick, 52, 55
Fielding, Herbert U., 144
Finley, David Edward, 132, 135
Finney, Ernest A., Jr., 150
Fireproof Building, 78

Fires, 126; *see also* Charleston, fires in
First Baptist Church, Columbia, 96
Fishdam Ford, Battle of, 55
Fishing Creek, 54
Fleming, C.E., 110
Floods, 119, 123
"Flora, or Hob in the Well," 26
Florence County, 111, 154
Florida, 2, 16
Floyd, John, 83
Folly Island, 82
Football, 111, 117, 138, 149
Force Bill, 83
Ford, Gerald, 146
Fort Caroline, 4
Fort Charlotte, 41, 47
Fort Dearborn, 69
Fort Granby, 56
Fort Jackson, 123, 132, 142
Fort Johnson, 18, 66
Fort King George, 21
Fort Loudoun, 33, 34
Fort Mechanic, 66
Fort Mill, 147
Fort Moore, 19, 41
Fort Motte, 56
Fort Moultrie, 53, 80, 86, 97
Fort Moultrie, Battle of, 48–49
Fort Prince George, 32, 34
Fort Pulaski, 103
Fort San Felipe, 4, 5
Fort Sumter, 81, 94, 97, 99, 100, 102
Fort Wagner, 99
Fort Watson, 55–56
Fourteenth Amendment, 103, 105
Fox, George, 12
Frankland, Thomas, 29, 30
Franklin, Benjamin, 57
Frazier, "Smokin' Joe," 142
Freedmen's Bureau, 102
French, 65; attacks by, 17

French Broad River, 3
French fleets, 52
French West Indies, 67
Friday's Ferry, 60
Friendly Society for the Mutual
Insuring of Houses against
Fire, 26, 29
Friendship Junior College, 138
Frogmore, 98
Fundamental Constitutions, 6–
7, 9, 11, 12, 14, 15
Furman University, 90, 91, 111,
141
"fusion" tickets, 118

Gadsden, Christopher, 35, 36,
39, 45, 48, 54, 57, 70
"gag rule," 85
Gaillard, John, 70
Gantt, Harvey, 116, 139
Garden, Dr. Alexander, 34
Garden, Rev. Alexander, 29
Garden, Alexander (d. 1829), 76
Garfield, James A., 109
Gary, Martin Witherspoon, 110
Gates, Horatio, 54
General Committee (1774), 45
General incorporation law, 111
General School Act, 106
Gent, Citizen, 66
George II, 24, 33
George III, 38, 44, 49
Georgetown, 3, 9, 23, 33, 43, 44,
55, 77, 101, 113, 150;
incorporated, 70; riots in, 118;
Washington visits, 65
Georgetown County, 69, 81, 139,
146
Georgia, 25, 31–32, 37
Georgia Convention, 49
German Colonization Society, 89
German Friendly Society, 40
German settlers, 25, 89
German Swiss settlers, 25
Gershwin, George, 143

Gibbes, Frances Guignard, 114
Gibbes, James S., 120
Gibbes Art Gallery, 120
Gibson, Althea, 137
Gillespie, "Dizzy," 123
Gillmore, Maj. Gen. Quincy A.,
102
Gillon, Alexander, 50, 53
Gilman, Caroline, 82
Glen, James, 29
Glorious Revolution, 13
Glover, Maggie, 154
Godbold, Lucile Ellerbe, 126
Goggins, Juanita W., 146
"The Gold Bug" (Poe), 80
Goldwater, Barry, 140
Golf, 60
Gonzalez, N.G., 112, 119
Goose Creek, 68
Goree, Janie Glymph, 147
Governor's Mansion, 104
Governor's School for Science
and Mathematics, 151
Governor's School for the Arts,
148
Grange, 106, 111
Graniteville Manufacturing
Company, 88
Grant, Lt. Col. James, 35
Grant, Ulysses S., 105, 106, 107
Granville, Lord, 23
Granville County, 18, 19
Gray, Wil Lou, 125
Grayson, William, 64, 91
Great Awakening, 28
Great Meadows (Va.), 32
Great Seal (royal), 47
Great Seal of S.C., 48, 50, 78
Great War for the Empire
(French and Indian War), 33,
36
Greenberg, Reuben, 149
Greene, Gen. Nathanael, 55, 56
Greenville, 90, 122, 134, 147,
153

Greenville Airport, 138
Greenville Baptist Female
  College, 91
Greenville County, 50, 59, 154
Greenville News, 107
Greenville Symphony, 135
Greenwood County, 117, 122
Gregg, William, 88
Grenville Packet (ship), 37
Grimk, Angelina, 81, 86
Grimk, John F., 76, 81
Grimk, Sarah, 76, 81, 86
Grimk, Thomas Smith, 84
Guerard, Peter Jacob, 13
Guignard, Jane Bruce, 122
Guignard, John Gabriel, 60
Guilford Court House (N.C.),
  Battle of, 55

Hamburg, 76, 107
Hamilton, Alexander, 66
Hamilton, James, 82, 83
Hammond, James H., 93
Hampton, Wade, III, 39, 75, 95,
  98, 100, 108, 109, 112, 119
Hampton County, 108, 121, 124
Hancock, John, 61
Hancock, Winfield S., 109
Hanging Rock, Battle of, 54
Harding, Warren G., 125
Harleston, Edwin A., 123
Harleston's Green, 60
Harper, Robert Goodloe, 39, 67
Harper, William, 84, 85
Harrington, James, 7
Harrison, Benjamin, 111
Harrison, William H., 87
Hart, Oliver, 47
Hartsville, 118, 120
Harvest Moon (ship), 102
Hawker, Capt. James, 41
Hayes, Rutherford B., 108
Hayne, Henry E., 107
Hayne, Isaac, 56
Hayne, Robert Y., 77, 80, 81, 83

Haynsworth, Clement, 143
Heath, Sir Robert, 5
Heath Patent, 5, 6
Heyward, Du Bose, 130
Heyward, Duncan Clinch, 95
Heyward, Thomas, Jr., 49, 51
Hibernian Society, 69
Higginson, Col. Thomas W., 99
Highland Park Hotel, 105
Highway commissioners, 130
Highway system, 127, 142
Hill, William, 53
Hilton, Capt. William, 5
Hilton Head, 6, 62, 73, 98
"The Hireling and the Slave"
  (Grayson), 91
*History of South-Carolina from
  its first Settlement in 1670, to
  the Year 1808* (Ramsay), 71
*History of the American
  Revolution* (Ramsay), 61
*History of the Revolution of
  South-Carolina, from a
  British Province to an
  Independent State* (Ramsay),
  58
Hoar, Samuel, 88
Hobcaw, 46
Hobcaw barony, 120
Hobkirk's Hill, 56
Hog Island channel, 47
Holderman, James B., 153
Hookworm, 115
Hoover, Herbert, 127
Horlbeck, John Aam, 41
Horlbeck, Peter, 41
Horry County, 69, 139
Housatonic, USS, 100
House of Representatives, U.S.,
  66, 85, 151, 154; speaker, 73,
  93
Howe, Gen. Robert, 51
Huck, Christian, 53, 54
Hudson, Charles, 2
Huger, Benjamin, 50

Huger, Daniel, 61
Huger, Gen. Isaac, 53
Huguenot Church, 13
Huguenots, 4, 11, 12
Hunley (submarine), 100
Huntington, Anna Vaughan
  Hyatt, 128
Huntington, Archer Milton, 128
Hurricanes, 32, 73, 77, 113, 121,
  132; Hugo, 152
Hutson, Richard, 51
Hyde, Edward (Earl of
  Clarendon), 5, 18

Imprints: first in state, 24
Incas, 1
Independent Company of British
  troops, 21, 22, 32
Indien (frigate), 53; *see also*
  South Carolina (frigate)
Indigo: as export of colony, 9;
  bounty on, 30; grown by Eliza
  Lucas Pinckney, 30; society
  formed, 33
Industrial Workers of the World,
  122
Influenza epidemic, 124
Inoculation, 27
Institute Hall, Charleston, 97
Insurance, 26, 67
Integration, 139, 141, 142, 144
Internal improvements, 74, 79
Interstate and West Indian
  Exposition, 118
Irby, John L.M., 112
Iron works, 45, 53
Iroquoian tribes, 2
Isaac Smith (gunboat), 99
Isle of Palms, 48
Izard, Sarah, 36

Jackson, Andrew, 41, 78, 80, 81,
  82
Jackson, "Shoeless" Joe, 125–
  126

Jacksonborough Assembly, 53,
  54, 57
"jail ins," 139
James II, 12, 13
James Island, 18
Jasper, Sgt. William, 49, 52
Jasper County, 121, 127
Jay, John, 57
Jay Treaty, 66
Jefferson, Thomas, 67, 69, 70, 81
Jenkins, Daniel Joseph, 150
Jenkinsville, 150
Jenrette, John, 148
Jeremiah, Thomas ("Jerry"), 47
Jews, 9, 14
Jillson, Justus K., 104
John Adams (sloop), 68
Johns, Jasper, 137
Johns Island, 52
Johnson, Andrew, 102
Johnson, David, 84
Johnson, I.S. Leevy, 144
Johnson, Judge William, 78
Johnson, Lyndon, 140
Johnson, Sir Nathaniel, 17, 18,
  24
Johnson, Robert, 21, 24
Johnson, William, 70
Johnston, Algernon Sidney, 91
Johnston, Henrietta Dering, 17
Johnston, Olin D., 130, 131, 133,
  139
Judicial districts, 43; Fifteenth,
  139; Sixteenth, 141; Twelfth,
  139

Kalb, Baron de, 50, 54
Kalteisen, Michael, 40
Kean, John, 61
Kennedy, John F., 138
Keowee, 32
Kershaw County, 65, 119
Kettle Creek, Battle of, 51
Kiawah Island, 145
"King Cotton," 93

King George's War (War of
Austrian Succession), 30, 31
King's Mountain, Battle of, 54,
55
King William's War, 13, 14
Kinsale, Ire., 7
Kirkland, Lane, 147
Knight-Ridder Company, 151
Koger Center for the Arts, 152

Labor: disputes, 122; hearings,
127; legislation, 112, 119, 123,
126; organizations, 66; "right
to work" legislation, 137
Lafayette, Marquis de, 50, 79
Lake City, 151
Lake Murray, 128
Lancaster County, 59, 147
Lander College, 119
Landis, Kenesaw Mountain,
126
Laudonniere, Rene de, 4
Laurens, Henry, 23, 35, 36, 39,
41, 42, 46, 48, 50, 51, 54–55,
57, 65
Laurens, John, 57
Laurens County, 59, 92
*Laws of the province of South
Carolina, The* (Trott), 26
Lawson's Fork, 45
Lee, Arthur, 46
Lee, Light Horse Harry, 55
Lee County, 119
Legar, James M., 63
Legareville, 99
Legislature, S.C., 52; origins of,
13–14; protests power of
federal government, 79; *see
also* Assembly, Commons
House of; Assembly, S.C.;
Council, S.C.
Leigh, Peter, 32
Lewisburg (Lexington) County,
59
Lexington (Mass.), 46

Lexington County, 25, 120, 128,
147
Libraries, 15
Lieber, Francis, 85
Lincoln, Abraham, 96, 97, 102
Lincoln, Benjamin, 53
Lining, Dr. John, 27
Linner, William, 73
Little River, 65
Little Tennessee River, 33
Local Government Act, 145
Locke, John, 6
London Philharmonic Orchestra,
152
Long Canes Creek, 34
Long Island. *See* Isle of Palms
Lords Proprietors, 5, 6, 9, 10, 11,
12, 13, 14, 18, 21, 23
Louis XIV, 12
Lowndes, Rawlins, 50
Lowndes, William, 72
Loyalists (Tories), 47, 48, 52;
property confiscated, 53, 54,
57
Lucas, Jonathan, 60
Ludwell, Phillip, 13, 14
Lumber, 8
Lunatic asylum, 76
Lutheran Church, 29
Lutherans, 93
Luxembourg, Chevalier de, 53
Lynch, Thomas, 39, 45
Lynch, Thomas, Jr., 49
Lynchings, 134
Lyttelton, William Henry, 33

McCord, David J., 85
McCormick County, 122
McCrady, Edward, 117
McDuffie, George, 83
Mace, 33
McKinley, William, 116, 118
McKnight, Marian, 137
Mack Trucks, 151
McLaurin, John L., 119

McNair, Ronald E., 151
Madison, James, 71, 72
Magazines (powder): seized, 46
Magrath, Andrew Gordon, 94,
96, 100, 103
Maham, Hezekiah, 56
Malaria, 8, 115
Mangum, Willie P., 85
Manning, Richard I., 95, 122,
123
Maps, 16
Margravate of Azilia, 20
Marion, Francis, 25, 38, 54, 55,
66
Marion County, 111, 121
Marlboro County, 59, 150
Mars Bluff, 42
Marshall, John, 67
Marshall, J.Q., 119
Mason, James, 98
Massachusetts: settlers from,
12, 14
Massachusetts Circular Letter,
42
Massacres, 4, 19, 34
Mathews, John, 51, 57
Maxwell, Cassandra, 132
Mayans, 1
Maybank, Burnet, 131
May chemical plant, 135
Mays, Benjamin E., 113
Means, John H., 91
Medical College of South
Carolina, 78
Medical College of the State of
South Carolina, 82
Medical Society of South
Carolina, 66
Medway, 12
Memminger, C.G., 92
Memoir on Slavery (Harper), 85
Memphis Commercial
Convention, 88
Mepkin plantation, 36, 65
Mercier, Lt. Peter, 32

Meteorology, 27
Methodist Church, 28
Methodists, 87, 90, 93, 110, 119
Mexican War, 88–89
Michelin Tire, 146
Middleburg, 15
Middleton, Arthur, 49
Middleton, Henry, 29, 45
Middleton, Thomas, 35
Middleton Place, 29
Midway (Ga.), 32
Military Academy, U.S., 106
Military government, 102, 103,
104
Militia, 107
Miller, Phineas, 69
Miller, Thomas E., 113, 116
Mills, 63; *see also* Textile mills;
Paper mills
Mills, Robert, 63, 76, 78, 87
Mills House, 100
The Mind of the South (Cash),
132
"Miss America," 137
Missionaries, 81, 98
"Miss Universe," 148
Mitchell, Theo, 153
Mobs, 85, 89, 134
Moderators, 43
Monaghan Mill, 122
Monck, George (Duke of
Albemarle), 5
Moncks Corner, 53
Money, 16, 23, 24, 46, 59
Monroe, James, 74, 76
Montagu, Gov. Lord Charles
Greville, 40, 44
Montgomery, Col. Archibald, 34
Montgomery, John H., 110
Montgomery, Sir Robert, 20
Moore, Daniel, 41
Moore, James, 16
Moore, James (son), 19, 21
Moore's Creek Bridge, Battle of,
48

Morgan, Daniel, 55
Morris Island, 97, 99
Moss, Joseph, 150
Motte, Rebecca, 56
Moultrie, William, 24, 48, 51, 52, 58, 70
Moultrieville, 74
Mount Pleasant, 127
Mount Vernon Ladies Association, 92
Mount Vernon Mills, 113
Muhlenberg, Heinrich Melchior, 29
Murray, George Washington, 114
Muschamp, George, 12
Muscogee (Ga.), 2
Musgrove's Mill, Battle of, 54
Muskhogean tribes, 5
Mutual Insurance Company, 67
Myrtle Beach, 2, 126, 144

NAACP, 123, 135
Nairne, Thomas, 17
Nashville Convention, 90
National Gallery of Art, 132
National Guard, 123, 130, 143
National Naval and Maritime Museum, 146
National Trust for Historic Preservation, 135
Nation Ford Treaty, 87
Native Americans (Indians): agents to, 17; and American Revolution, 46; as slaves, 5, 16, 18; culture of, 1–2; origins of, 1; population, 10, 18; trade with, 8, 18; *see also* Algonquian tribes; Appalachee Indians; Aztecs; Catawba Indians; Cheraw Indians; Cherokee Indians; Chickasaw Indians; Choctaw Indians; Creek Indians; Incas; Iroquoian tribes; Mayans;

Muskhogean tribes; Shawnee Indians; Siouan tribes; Westos tribes
Natural History of Carolina, Florida and the Bahama Islands (Catesby), 22
Naturalization law, 58
Naval Academy, U.S., 107
Naval stores, 18
Navigation laws, British, 12, 24
Navy, British, 28, 30, 47, 48, 57
The Negro Law of South Carolina (O'Neall), 89
Nelson, Annie Greene, 132
New Acquisition District, 53
Newberry College, 93
Newberry County, 59, 150
Newcastle (Pa.), 26
New England Society of Charleston, 75
Newfoundland, 2
New Ironsides, USS, 100
Newman, I. DeQuincy, 149
Newspapers. *See Charleston Courier; Columbia Record; Fairfax Enterprise; Greenville News; Pendleton Messenger; Charleston Post and Courier; The State; State Gazette of South-Carolina*
Niagara, USS, 98
Nicholson, Francis, 21, 22
Niernsee, John R., 92
Nightingale, HMS, 36
Nineteenth Amendment, 125
Ninety Six, 43, 44, 47, 59; siege of, 56
Nixon, Richard, 142, 144
Nobel Prize, 140
Nonexportation agreement, 47
Nonimportation agreements, 43, 44, 45
North Carolina, 37; as distinct from S.C., 13, 14, 18;

boundary with, 25, 26;
governed as part of S.C., 8
Northeastern Railroad depot
(Charleston), 101
North Island, 77
Nova Scotia, 33
Nuclear power plants, 139, 150
Nullification, 81, 82; Ordinance
of, 83
Nullification Convention, 83

Oaths, 49, 84
Ocean Forest Hotel, 126
Ocmulgee (Ga.), 2
Oconee County, 50, 104
Oglethorpe, James, 25, 28, 29
Olympia Mill, 113
O'Neall, John Belton, 84, 89, 93
Operas, 26
Operation Jackpot, 149
Operation Lost Trust, 152, 153
Opportunity School, 125
Orangeburg, 43, 44, 56, 105, 109
Orangeburg County, 120
Orangeburg township, 25
Orange parish, 51
Orange trees, 31
The Orphan (Otway), 26
Orphanage, Jenkins', 150
Orr, James L., 93, 103, 105
Osceola, 86
Otway, Thomas, 26
Owens Field airport, 127
Oyster Point, 11

Packetboat service, 37
Pacolet Manufacturing
Company, 110
Pacolet River, 45, 119
Paine, Thomas, 48
Palmer, Col. John, 23
Palmetto Day, 50
Palmetto flag, 89
Palmetto Regiment, 88, 89
Palmetto State (ironclad), 101

Palmetto tree: as state symbol,
49
Paper mills, 149
Pardo, Juan, 4
Parishes: as units of
representation, 22
Parker, Alton B., 119
Parker, Lewis, 122
Parker, Sir Peter, 48
Parliament, British, 17, 24, 30,
39, 40, 43
Parris Island, 4, 112
Parr Shoals, 139
Patents, 13
Patriots Point, 146
Patterson, Elizabeth, 151
Payne, Daniel A., 81, 84, 101
Peace Center for the Performing
Arts, 153
Peace Island plantation, 60
Peace of Ryswick, 14
Pee Dee region, 26
Pee Dee River, 42
Pellagra, 115
Pelzer, Francis, 110
Pelzer Manufacturing Company,
110
Pendleton, Nathaniel, 39
Pendleton District, 74, 79
Pendleton Farmers' Society, 73
Pendleton Messenger, 81
Penn Normal and Industrial
School, 98
Pennsylvania, 8; settlers from,
39
People's State Bank, 128
Peronneau, Samuel, 37
Perry, Benjamin F., 102
Perry, James M. "Miss Jim,"
124
Perry, Matthew J., 147
Peterkin, Julia, 127
Petigru, James L., 92, 99
"Philolethes" (Henry Laurens),
35

"Philopatrios" (Christopher
Gadsden), 35
Phoenix, 118
Phosphates, 103
Pickens, Andrew, 27, 39, 52, 74
Pickens, Francis W., 94
Pickens County, 50, 79, 107, 134
Pierce, Franklin, 91
Pinckney, Charles (d. 1758), 30,
32, 33
Pinckney, Charles (d. 1782), 45,
46
Pinckney, Charles (d. 1824), 33,
38, 39, 59–60, 68, 75, 78; at
constitutional convention, 61
Pinckney, Charles Cotesworth,
30, 33, 38, 61, 67, 68, 70, 71,
79
Pinckney, Eliza Lucas, 30
Pinckney, Henry Laurens, 85
Pinckney, Thomas, 31, 33, 67,
80
Pirates, 8, 20, 21
Pitt, William: statue of, 44
Planter (steamship), 98
Plays, 16, 26
Plessy v. *Ferguson*, 116, 117
Poe, Edgar Allan, 80
Poetry Society, 125
Poinsett, Joel R., 79, 86
Poinsettia, 79
Polk, James K., 88
Pollitzer, Carrie T., 110
Pope, Joseph D., 110
Pope John Paul II, 151
Population (census), 8, 11, 15,
18, 21, 23, 28, 31, 34, 43, 52,
62, 68, 71–72, 75, 81, 86, 90,
96, 105, 109, 112, 118, 120,
125, 126, 128, 132, 135, 138,
143, 147–148, 152–153
Porgy, 130
Porgy and Bess, 141, 143
Port Royal (ship), 7, 9
Port Royal County, 18

Port Royal Island, Battle of, 51
Port Royal Sound, 4, 10, 18, 98
Portuguese, 31
Potter, Gen. Edward, 102
Preservation, 86, 125, 128
Prevost, Augustine, 52
Primogeniture, 65
Prince Frederick parish, 25, 33
Prince George Winyah parish,
22, 25, 41
Prince William parish, 30
Printing press, 24
Privy Council, British, 21, 23
Progressive Democratic Party,
133
Prohibition, 122
"A Prospect of Charlestown"
(engraving), 27
Provincial Congress: First, 45–
46; Second, 47, 48
PTL (Praise the Lord), 151
Pulaski, Comte, 52
Pulitzer Prize, 127
Purry, Jean Pierre, 25
Purrysburg, 25, 30

Quakers, 12, 14, 71
Queen Anne's War, 16, 19
Queen of Confitachiqui, 2
Quitrents, 24

Radio stations, 128
Railroads, 74, 84, 87, 91
Rainey, Joseph H., 106
Rambo, 113
Ramsay, David, 39, 58, 61, 69,
71, 73
Randolph (frigate), 50
Ransier, Alonzo J., 106
Rantowle's Bridge, Battle near,
52
Ratification convention, 61
Ravenel, Charles D. "Pug," 145
Rawdon, Col. Francis, Lord, 56
Reagan, Ronald, 148, 150

Reconstruction, 94–95
The Recruiting Officer, 26, 131
Reform Judaism, 79
Regiments, 1st SC Volunteers,
 98–99
Regiments, 54th Mass., 99
Regiments, S.C. Provincial, 35
Regulation, plan of, 42
Regulators, 40, 41, 43, 44;
 proclamation to suppress, 42
Religious toleration, 7, 9
Republican Party, 139, 146, 149
Resorts, 68, 145
*The Revised Statutes of South
 Carolina*, 106
Revolution of 1719, 21
Revolution of 1890, 112
Rhett, Robert Barnwell, 88, 90,
 91
Rhett, Sarah, 29
Rhett, Col. William, 17, 20, 29
Ribaut, Jean, 4
Rice, 8; as state's leading staple,
 58; and British navigation
 laws, 17, 24; commercial
 production ends, 121; early
 cultivation, 10–11, 12;
 excluded from nonexportation
 agreement, 47; machines, 13;
 Madagascar, 11; tidal mill for,
 60
Richardson, Col. Richard, 48
Richland County, 59, 86, 149
Richmond (ship), 11
Riley, Joseph P., Jr., 146
Riley, Richard, 150, 154
Riots, 131; election, 118; over
 liquor laws, 113; race, 107,
 118
Rivers Bridge, Battle of, 101
Riviera Theater, 131
Roanoke River, 1
Robert, Henry Martyn, 108
Roberts, Bishop, 27
Robert Y. Hayne (train), 87

Robinson, Jackie, 138
Rock Hill, 122, 138, 147
Rocky Mount, 69
Rogers, George, 149
Rogers, Moses, 75
Roosevelt, Franklin D., 115, 128,
 130, 132, 133, 134
Roosevelt, Theodore, 119
Rose, HMS, 29, 30
*The Rose Bud, or Youth's
 Gazette*, 82
Round O, 56
Royal, C.C., 145
"Runnin' Wild," 126
Rural Carolinian, 105
Russell, Donald S., 139
Rutledge, Edward, 31, 45, 49,
 51, 68
Rutledge, John, 27, 38, 39, 45,
 48, 50, 51, 52, 61, 66, 67, 68

St. Andrews Hall, Charleston,
 89, 97
St. Andrew's parish, 17, 20
St. Andrew's Society, 23
St. Augustine (Fla.), 23, 27, 54;
 as threat to S.C., 4, 5, 10, 29;
 attacked, 16, 28
St. Bartholomew's parish, 17,
 92
St. Cecilia Society, 35
St. David's parish, 42
St. George's Dorchester parish,
 20
St. George's Society, 25
St. Helena Island, 98
St. Helena's parish, 19, 41
St. James's Goose Creek parish,
 17
St. James's Santee parish, 17,
 22, 32
St. John's Berkeley parish, 17
St. John's Colleton parish, 25
St. John's River (Fla.), 4, 27
St. Luke's parish, 41, 88

St. Mark's Episcopal Church, 101
St. Mark's parish, 33
St. Mary's Church, 65
St. Matthew's parish, 42, 51
St. Michael's church, 11, 32, 35, 66, 67
St. Michael's parish, 31
St. Paul's parish, 17, 25, 36
St. Peter parish, 30
St. Philip's church, 11, 22, 28, 67, 84, 90
St. Philip's parish, 17, 31
St. Simons Island, 29
St. Stephen parish, 32
St. Thomas and St. Denis parish, 17
Salkehatchie, 19
Saluda County, 116
Saluda Manufacturing Company, 84
Saluda River, 110, 128
Sampit River, 23
Sandford, Capt. Robert, 6
San Marcos, 5
San Miguel de Gualdape, 3
Santee, High Hills of, 56
Santee Canal Company, 60
Santee-Cooper project, 131, 133
Santee River, 55–56, 60
Santo Domingo (W.I.), 2, 3, 64
Sardoine, HMS, 41
Savannah (Ga.), 25, 51, 52, 75, 103; Lafayette visits, 79; Sherman and, 94, 100; Washington visits, 65
Savannah River, 1, 3, 18, 19, 25, 25, 41, 47, 76
Savannah River Plant, 136
Saxe-Gotha township, 25
Saxton, Gen. Rufus, 101
Sayle, Col. William, 9, 10
Scarlet Sister Mary (Peterkin), 127

Schools, 70, 92; for blacks, 29; free, 19, 72; segregated, 136
Schultz, Henry, 76
Scotland, 17
Scots, 12, 17, 23
Scott, Robert K., 104, 105
Scott, Sir Walter, 82
Screven, Elisha, 23
Sea Islands, 98, 101, 124
Seamen Acts, 77–78, 88
Secession: Convention, 94, 96–97; Ordinance of, 97
Secessionville, 98
Secretary of Education, U.S., 154
Segregation, 95, 115–116, 117; challenged in court, 135; opposition to, 124
Senate, U.S., 67, 70, 74, 80, 91, 92, 128
Shannon, W.M., 109
Shaw, Robert Gould, 99
Shawnee Indians, 19
"Shell Manifesto," 112
Sherman, Gen. William T., 84, 94, 100, 101
Shipwrecks, 7, 9
Shute's Folly, 66
Sickles, Maj. Gen. Daniel E., 103, 104
Sidney Park, Columbia, 91
Simkins, Modjeska Montieth, 118
Simms, William Gilmore, 64, 84, 106
Simons, Benjamin, 15
Simpson, Merton D., 150
Singleton, Angelica, 86, 87
Singleton, Richard, 86
Siouan tribes, 2, 3
"sit-ins," 138
"6-0-1" school law, 126
Slave revolts, 3, 24, 27, 40, 64, 74, 77, 89
Slavery, 8, 63–64, 71, 87, 88;

defended, 85; laws, 13, 14, 22, 28, 69, 76; opposition to, 73, 76, 81
Slaves, 15, 57; African, 8, 27; and American Revolution, 46; de facto freemen, 98; emancipation of, 69, 103; first in English Carolina, 10; Native Americans as, 5, 16, 18; population, 8, 15, 18, 21, 23, 28, 31, 34, 43, 52, 62, 68, 71–72, 75, 86, 95; provisions for, 39
Slave trade, 28, 40, 60, 63, 70, 71
Slidel, John, 98
Sloane, Sir Hans, 22
Smallpox, 27, 34, 69, 97
Smalls, Robert, 98
Smith, Alfred E., 127
Smith, Ellison Durant ("Cotton Ed"), 120, 130, 131
Smith, James W., 106
Smith, Landgrave Thomas, 12
Smith, Landgrave Thomas (second), 23
Smith, Robert, 67
Smith, William, 74, 77
Smith, William Loughton, 39, 66
Smith v. *Allwright*, 133
Smyth, Ellison, 110
Social Security Act, 130
Society for the Preservation of Old Dwellings, 125
Society for the Propagation of Christian Knowledge, 15
Society for the Propagation of the Gospel in Foreign Parts, 16
Sonoco Products, 118
Sons of Liberty, 70
Sothell, Seth, 14
South Carolina (frigate), 53; *see also Indien* (frigate)

South Carolina Academy of Fine Arts, 76, 78, 81
South Carolina Athletic Hall of Fame, 126
South Carolina Bar, 146
South Carolina Bar Association, 80, 118, 146
South Carolina Bench and Bar (Brooks), 120
South Carolina Canal and Rail Road Company, 80
South Carolina College, 64, 70, 75, 80, 84, 85, 87
South Carolina Cotton Manufactory, 73
South Carolina Educational Television (SCETV), 138
South Carolina Federation of Colored Women's Clubs, 121
South-Carolina Gazette, 25, 28, 35
South Carolina Golf Club, 60
South Carolina Hall of Fame, 144
South Carolina Historical Society, 92
South Carolina National Bank, 153
South Carolina Navy, 50
South Carolina Philharmonic Orchestra, 136
South Carolina Public Welfare Act, 130
South Carolina Society, 31
South Carolina State College, 142
South Caroliniana Society, 130
South Edisto River, 5
Southern campaign (Rev.), 51
Southern Review, 80
Southern Rights Association, 90
Spanish, 28, 29, 31; attacks by, 10, 13, 17; war against, 36
Spanish-American War, 117
Spanish missions, 5

Spartanburg, 73, 87, 90, 147
Spartanburg County, 59
Special Field Order No. 15, 101
Speights, A. M., 107
Spoleto Festival, 146
Stamp Act, 39, 40, 44
Stamp Act Congress, 39
Star of the West (ship), 97
The State, 112, 119
State Agricultural and
    Mechanical Society, 111
State Bank, 69
State Bar Association, 142
State Board of Charities and
    Corrections, 122
State Board of Health, 109
State Board of Law Examiners,
    121
State Budget and Control
    Board, 135
Stateburg, 87
State College for Negroes, 116
State Department of Parks,
    Recreation and Tourism, 141
State Development Board, 131
State ex rel. George v. Aiken, 113
State Fair, 92, 144
State flower (yellow jessamine),
    126
State Forestry Commission, 127
*State Gazette of South-
    Carolina*, 58
State Highway Department,
    123, 130
State Highway Patrol, 128
State Historical Commission,
    113
State House (Charleston), 32,
    46, 61
State House (Columbia), 61, 91,
    92, 108, 139
State Museum, 113, 152
State Penitentiary, 131
State Planning Board, 131
State Ports Authority, 132

State Railroad Commission, 109
State-Record Company, 151
State Road, the, 80
State song ("Carolina"), 121
States' Rights Party, 134
State Tax Commission, 122
State tree (palmetto), 131
*The Statutes at Large of South
    Carolina* (Cooper and
    McCord), 85
Stevenson, Adlai, 136, 137
Stevensons, Nancy, 146
Stevenson v. West, 145
"stone fleet," 98
Stono River, 27, 52
Stuart, J. E. B., 100
Stuart, Capt. John, 34, 36, 37
Stuart's Town, 12, 13
Suffrage, 72; property
    qualifications, 22
Sugar, 63
Sullivan's Island, 49, 68, 74, 80
Summer Nuclear Station, V. C.,
    150
Sumner, Charles, 92
Sumter, Thomas, 25, 38, 54, 55,
    56, 82
Sumter County, 68, 87, 119
Superintendent of Education,
    104
Superintendent of Indian
    Affairs, 36, 37
Superintendent of Public Works,
    74
Supreme Court, S.C., 105, 150,
    151
Supreme Court, U.S., 67, 70,
    128, 132, 133, 137, 143, 145
Swamp Angel, 100
Swinton, William, 23
Swiss settlers, 25
Sword of State, 17

Taft, William H., 120
Tailfer, Patrick, 29

Tamar, HMS, 47
Tar, 8
Tariffs, 82, 83
Tarleton, Col. Banastre, 52, 53, 54, 55
Taxes, 23, 28, 40, 57, 79; sales, 136, 150; state income, 117
Taylor, James, 60
Taylor, Thomas, 60
Taylor, Zachary, 89
Tea Act, 45
Technical education program, 139
Telegraph, 89
Television, 136, 138
Tennent, William, 47
Tennessee River, 3
Tennis, 137
Textile mills, 73, 88, 95, 103, 110, 112, 113, 122, 126
Thatch (Teach), Edward, 20
Theaters, 26, 125, 131
Theodora (ship), 98
Thirteenth Amendment, 103
Thomas, Samuel, 16
Thompson, William, 49
Three Brothers (ship), 9
Thurmond, Strom: elected governor, 134; elected to Senate in write-in campaign, 137; joins Republican Party, 140; presidential candidate of States Rights' party, 134
Tillman, Benjamin Ryan, 89, 95, 111, 112, 119; death of, 124; elected to U.S. Senate, 113
Tillman, James H., 119
Timothy, Ann, 28
Timothy, Ann Donovan, 58
Timothy, Lewis, 26, 28
Timrod, Henry, 121
Toal, Jean H., 151
Tobacco, 10, 39, 44, 76, 77
Tornadoes, 131, 150
Tourism, 105, 113, 141

Tower of London, 54–55
Townes, Charles, 140
Townshend duties, 43
Town Theater, 125
Treaty of Augusta, 37
Treaty of Madrid, 10
Treaty of Paris (1763), 36, 37
Treaty of Paris (1783), 58
Treaty of Utrecht, 19
Tricentennial, 141, 143
Trott, Nicholas, 26
A True and Historical Narrative (Tailfer, Anderson, et al.), 29
Truman, Harry, 134
Tubman, Harriet, 99
Turnbull, Robert J., 80, 83
Turpentine, 8
Tuscarora Indians, 18, 19
"Twenty-six," the, 43
Tybee Island (Ga.), 52
Tyger River, 55
Tyler, John, 87

Union Camp corporation, 149
Union County, 59
United Daughters of the Confederacy, 113
University of South Carolina, 69, 107, 114, 116, 117, 138, 149, 153; Alumni Association, 110; anti-war demonstrations at, 143; integration of, 139; law school, 110, 124, 136, 145; segregated, 109
University of South Carolina Press, 121, 133
Vaccination, 69
Van Buren, Abram, 86
Van Buren, Martin, 85, 86, 87
Verrazzano, Giovanni da, 2
Vesey, Denmark, 77
Vice Admiralty Court, S.C., 48
Virginia, 8, 37; settlers from, 39
Voorhees, Ralph, 117

Voorhees Normal and Industrial
  School, 117
Voting Rights Act, 116, 141

Waccamaw River, 3
Waddel, Moses, 70
Wagener, John A., 89
Walhalla, 89
Walker, N.P., 87
Wambaw (sloop), 41
Wando River, 17
War Hawks, 72
Waring, Waites, 134
War of Jenkins' Ear, 27
Washington, George, 32, 61;
  visits S.C., 65
Washington, Col. William, 52
Wateree River, 2, 3
The Water is Wide (Conroy), 144
Watson, Albert, 143
Waxhaws, 41, 53
WCSC (radio), 128
WCSC (television), 136
Weather, 3, 30–31, 144; *see also*
  Hurricanes; Tornadoes
Weatherly, Shawn, 148
Weaver, Philip, 73
Webster, Daniel, 81, 89
Weems, Parson, 79, 82
Weld, Theodore, 86
Welsh settlers, 26
Welsh Tract, 26
Wesley, John, 26
West, John, 126, 143
West, Joseph, 7, 10, 11
West Columbia, 127
Westos tribes, 5, 11
Whitefield, George, 28
Whitmarsh, Thomas, 25
Whitney, Eli, 66, 69
Who Speaks for the South?
  (Dabbs), 140
Wilkes, John, 43, 44
William, Maj. Andrew, 48
William and Mary, 13

William & Ralph (ship), 10
William III of England, 13, 15
Williams, David R., 72
Williams, Mary, 29
Williamsburg County, 59, 111
Williamson, Maj. Andrew, 47, 49
Williamson's Plantation, Battle
  of, 54
Willington, 70
Wilmot Proviso, 88
Wilson, John Lyde, 86
Wilson, Woodrow, 121, 123
Wilton, Joseph, 44
Wimbledon (Eng.), 137
Windmill Point, 18
Winnsborough, 59
Winthrop Normal College for
  Women, 113
Winton (Edgefield), 59
Winyah Indigo Society, 33
Wofford, Benjamin, 90
Wofford, William, 45
Wofford College, 90, 111
Women: admitted to University,
  114; as editors, 28, 58, 118; on
  bench, 151; elected to
  statewide office, 146; in law,
  124, 132; in legislature, 127;
  in medicine, 113, 117; in
  sports, 126, 137; in U.S.
  House of Representatives, 151
Women's Christian Temperance
  Union, 109
Women's Rights, 110, 118, 122,
  124, 125, 141
Woodmason, Charles, 40
Woodside, John T., 126
Workman, William D., Jr.,
  139
World War I, 123, 124
World War II, 131, 134
WPA, 131
Wragg, William, 33, 40
Wright, Elizabeth Evelyn, 117
Wright, Jonathan Jasper, 105

XYZ Affair, 67, 68

Yamacraw Bluff, 25
Yarmouth, HMS, 50
Yawkey, Thomas A., 146
Yeamans, Sir John, 6, 9, 11
Yeamans, William, 6
Yellow fever, 15, 17

The Yemassee (Simms), 84
Yemassee Indians, 19, 20, 23
Yemassee War, 17, 19, 20
York County, 59, 147, 151
York District, 87
Yorktown, USS, 146
Young, Virginia Durant, 118